TOP DOGS
AND THEIR PETS

For Jodi —
you of all people know
this was a true labor of
love. Lots of miles, lots of
hours, and lots of hours.
Thank you for your support
and interest along the way.
Enjoy!
Best wishes, David and Suji

Photography by
David Woo and Richard Michael Pruitt

Foreword by Diane Rehm

Parapet Press

Copyright © 2009 Parapet Press • ISBN: 978-0-9841086-0-2

Published by Parapet Press
an imprint of Pediment Publishing
Battle Ground, WA
parapetpress.com

Dedication

I wish to thank a wonderful group of family and friends whose support gave me the strength to complete this book: Suzi Woo, who gave me direction, and shared with me the immense gift of support as we travelled repeatedly all over our great country, working long hours, and living out of a suitcase. For my children: Zach, for helping me on photo shoots when Suzi could not travel to the Austin and San Antonio areas; Jake, for assisting us with the photograph of Former President George Herbert Bush and his dog Sadie, and for serving our country in the army in Iraq; and Carrie, for assisting with the photo shoot of Sully Sullenberger with his dog. Thank you to Hilary Bowerman and Shelby Poole, for giving up their mother's time, so she could travel and be my collaborator on the book; and my two grandsons, Walker and Hughes Bowerman, for sharing their grandmother for two years. I give special thanks to my wonderful parents, who gave me the inspiration and the freedom to pursue my passion of photography, and especially to my father, for allowing me to make photographs with his prized Leica camera when I was 10 years old. Last, but not least, to all the pet rescue people and organizations that spend time and resources in helping all no-kill animal shelters and breed-specific rescue groups.

David Woo

I dedicate this book to the people that work and volunteer at animal shelters and remind others that people who mistreat animals will, sooner than later, mistreat people.

Richard Michael Pruitt

Acknowledgments

I could not have completed this book without the help and understanding of so many people. Where do I start? Many thanks go to my wife, Suzi, for giving me Chester, my five-year-old Bassett hound, as a birthday gift. The book would have taken another four and a half years to finish without her help. Suzi videotaped nearly all of the photo sessions which you may view at: www.topdogspets.com. As a team, we edited and made the final decisions for the format and design of the publication. She worked long hours zigzagging across the U. S. on photo shoots, and she was fully responsible for gathering and processing all of the Q & A's for all ninety-two of our subjects.

My gratitude goes to Brad Fenison, President of Pediment Publishing ,and his entire staff for helping make the book possible. Special thanks to Justin McCullough, Director of Business Development at Pediment, for direction in marketing and development of the book. After hours of long conversations and hundreds of e-mails and phone calls, these two men came to Dallas one weekend to talk about how they could help me produce and market our book. I remember sitting in the lobby of a hotel, with our three laptops and notepads, mapping out a timeline and market-ing plan, and thinking how lucky I was to have a publisher that shared my vision.

When I met Diane Rehm for the first time at WMAU radio station in Washington, D.C., I was overwhelmed by how approachable and friendly she was. I remain a longtime fan and listener of her show, *The Diane Rehm Show.* I knew she owned a dog, Maxie, and I asked if she would pose for me. We went back to Washington a few months later to photograph her and at that point I knew she would be the perfect person to write the forward for the book.

It was a cool and rainy day when Suzi and I pulled up in front of Cesar and Ilusion Millan's home in California. We are big fans of his TV show and we were anxious to finally meet the Millan's. The visit began with an introduction to their two sons, in addition to Daddy and around seven other dogs. I could sense the compassion they had for their pets and their commitment to rescue animals. We are thrilled to have Cesar and his pets featured on the cover and inside the book.

Jan Miller, literary agent and dear friend, and one of the ninety-one "top dogs," was very helpful in so many ways. She and her staff, and especially Lauren Shults, were instrumental in facilitating several important contacts for *Top Dog* subjects. Her dog, Schumacher, a very cute and obedient beagle, was the best pet we photographed, posing like a true model himself beside Jan. Okay, Cesar, your dogs were a very close second.

I owe a great deal of gratitude to Barbara Buzzell, president of The Buzzell Company, and Maggie Raymond. Barbara and I have been friends for many years, and, thankfully, she did not hesitate when I asked her to be my publicist. Barbara and Maggie did an awesome job updating the press release, and introducing me to the right contact people at Neiman Marcus.

Thanks go to Callie Storz, a buyer for Neiman Marcus, and Shannon Nunez, assistant buyer for Neiman Marcus for showcasing *Top Dogs* in the prestigious *Neiman Marcus Christmas Book*. Thank you also to Bill Makin, vice president of Neiman Marcus for all of his help in promoting our project.

Thanks to Louis DiCenzo, a longtime friend and a publicist for *The Dr. Phil Show,* for his perseverance and assistance with scheduling Jay McGraw, producer of the new TV show, *The Doctors.*

Thanks also to Shannon Powers, a publicist who was greatly helpful in securing "top dogs" in the L. A. area.

My sincere gratitude goes to David Guzman, a talented young video editor, for spending hours looking through more than seventy-five videos and editing them down to about one minute each. These entertaining pieces are behind-the-scene peeks at our photo shoots.

Last, but not least, thanks to Robert Decherd, chairman of the board, president and CEO of the A. H. Belo Corporation, for giving me his blessing, and for posing with his dog. Thanks also to the following staff of *The Dallas Morning News:* Jim Moroney, publisher/CEO; Bob Mong, editor; George Rodrique, managing editor; Walt Stallings, senior deputy managing editor; Leslie White, director of photography; and Irwin Thompson and Chris Wilkins, assistant directors of photography; and to Gary Barber and Ahna Hubnik, for their friendship and technical support.

David Woo

Foreword

When I think about Maxie, I smile. His are the wagging tail and soft belly that greet me when I walk in the door. Or the furry ball that huddles next to me when lightning and thunder crash in the night. Or the quiet pup under my desk, waiting for me to get off the air. He adores me. And I adore him. He's an incredibly important part of my life, and that of my husband, John.

All of the "top dogs" you will meet in this book feel the same way about the creatures they live with. They are, often as not, thought of as "friends," as well as "pets." Realizing that anthropomorphizing is not what we should be doing with our pets, I find it nevertheless difficult – if not impossible – to think of Maxie as anything other than a dear friend.

Maxie makes me laugh, he looks at me with adoring eyes, he stays by my side, we share meals, and, when I am sick, he kisses my face and comforts me. What else are dear friends for?

What is it about these wonderful beings that fill us with such joy, whether they are dogs, cats, horses, roosters, or even mules? I would suggest they add a richness and dimension to our lives that are, perhaps, not available to us in our interactions with other human beings. In fact, I believe our interactions with these creatures make us better human beings, more understanding, more open to the joys and heartaches of life.

Dogs have been the primary pets in my life, though cats have played a pretty important role as well. Throughout my childhood, there were several dogs: a black Fox Terrier, a brown-and-white Terrier, and a honey-colored Cocker Spaniel. There were no cats in our home, and, in fact, I felt no great love for cats. But shortly after my husband and I married, a friend persuaded me to take a male kitten from her cat's litter. Before a week had passed, I had become so enamored with the tiny creature that we went back to my friend and asked for another male. We gave them Arabic names: Imshe (meaning "walk" or "move"), and Jibne (meaning "cheese"). The two were inseparable until they died. It was only after my mother-in-law visited us and saw how delighted we were with the two kittens that she confessed how worried she'd been about her new daughter-in-law because she didn't love cats!

And then there was Cricket, an emaciated Calico cat who came limping down the street while we were vacationing at Ocean City. I'd promised the children they could have a new kitten, but I had something special in mind, like a purebred Persian. This poor little thing had watery eyes and a bitten-off tail, and was surely filled with fleas. Not in my house, I declared. But of course, my daughter begged her dad and he in turn persuaded me. So home with us came little Cricket, the vet declaring when he first saw her that she'd likely be dead in a week. He was utterly astounded when he saw her again two weeks later, looking perky, shiny, and healthy, the result of our son, David, sleeping on the floor with her for the first few nights, making sure she had enough to eat and drink. Cricket gave us many litters that friends of ours came to love and enjoy.

Later came our first dog, Katinka, a long-haired purebred Dachshund. At the time she came into our home, our daughter, Jennifer, had begun learning to ride horses, and became quite good at jumping. So, with the help of her father, Jennie created a mini-version of a steeplechase in the garden, and trained Katinka to jump the hoops as she ran around holding her by the leash. A dear and indulgent dog, indeed.

I've often wondered whether people have pets they resemble. Looking at the photo of Shirley Jones with her golden-haired Labrador, I can believe it. They are so beautiful together, and reflect each other's posture, warmth, and style. Even their eyes share the same light! And look at Ty Murray atop his horse, Grey! The two mirror each other perfectly!

Then there are the habits these creatures inflict upon us, or perhaps, we allow them to inflict on us. I'm thinking about artist Vernon Fisher, whose cat lies across his newspaper, presumably to prevent Vernon from reading it. When I get in bed each night, I look forward to reading novels, just for pleasure. If Maxie wants attention, he'll get onto my stomach, and gently push at the book, until I put it down to pet him. And, of course, I do!

I laughed as I read about Isaac Mizrahi! He named his dog Harry, he said, because it's a happy dog and "also because it is close to the word HAIRY, which Harry is very." Isaac, too, looks very happy and hairy!

Finally, while the majority of us choose to share our lives with dogs, cats, or horses, you will see that Bob Wade has capped his dome with a favorite creature having sharp toenails. To each his own, I say, and whether they have sharp claws, bark at the neighbors, dig in the garden, or screech in the night, we, the "top dogs," are very fortunate to live with the pets we love.

Diane Rehm
May 23, 2009
Washington, D.C.

Preface

Of course there are dogs, 107 of them; labs and terriers and various canine multi-ethnics included—along with eight cats, a few horses, and a handful of fish—but who would have thought that when David Woo and Richard Michael Pruitt set out across the country, intent on photographing alpha humans and their animal sidekicks, that they would find a bearded dragon, a pig, a snake, and an eagle?

Many things, it turns out, are unpredictable in the shared world of creatures and people. *Top Dogs and Their Pets* brings us more than its share of unexpected revelations and riddles.

The naming process, alone, has its mysteries. For example, hockey star Mike Modano named his lab, Bear, after an athlete—but not another hard-charger on skates. Instead, he picked the nickname of a gentlemanly golfer. Singer/Songwriter Lisa Loeb christened her cat, Chinchy Morty, because, well, she more or less explains that on page 52. And if you think actor Owen Wilson named his avocado-eating Blue Heeler, Garcia, for the famous Grateful Dead front man, you're among the mistaken multitudes.

Other inside info: The black Lab, belonging to NFL Hall-of-Famer Roger Staubach has a thing for Starbucks Pumpkin Bread. According to Laura Bush, former First Dog, Barney, acts like a Secret Service agent. Rodeo legend Ty Murray wishes his horse, Grey, could fly.

By the way, if Murray couldn't have a horse as a pet, he might choose an elephant— a bull-rider on a pachyderm might make a pretty good picture.

In these ninety-one black-and-white portraits, Woo and Pruitt have captured, with eloquent simplicity, the bond that joins pets and their owners. One glance at any of these photographs and the reader will see that this bond goes both ways. We care for them and they comfort us. We provide the food and they, the entertainment. They give us devoted companionship and we give them shoes to chew.

Look closely at some of these photos and you may see that a certain resemblance has begun to emerge between people and their furry companions. And who really began to look like whom first? Who has the greenest eyes, Olympic gymnast Carly Patterson, or her cat, Beijing? Did David Woo develop that soulful gaze before or after Chester came into his life? See his portrait by Steve Miller, who is also featured in the book.

Some pets go beyond mere resemblance and adopt the traits of their human friends. Race car driver Ashley Force says her cat, Simba, can "skid sideways through a room." Motivational speaker Zig Ziglar insists his Welsh Corgi has an uncanny ability to "persuade my wife to give her more food."

Lots of us wish our pets could talk to us. The artist Rosson Crow wishes her Shih-Tzu could speak with a French accent. And if they could talk, what would they say? Probably, they would urge us to buy this book.

That's because part of the proceeds from the sale of *Top Dogs and Their Pets* will benefit the Cesar and Ilusion Millan Foundation. This national nonprofit group helps animal shelters in the rescue, rehabilitation, and placement of abused and abandoned dogs. It also supports organizations committed to saving dogs from euthanasia.

It's an important thing to consider during those shared early-morning walks, Frisbee sessions in the yard, outings to the lake, or snowy nights around the fireplace. We might ask ourselves what we can do for animals because we already know what they do for us.

The final word on that comes from Jerry Jeff Walker; the great singer/songwriter summed up the spirit of *Top Dogs and Their Pets* when he was asked to list his dog's best asset.

Jerry Jeff's answer: "Her undying love."

Doug Swanson

Table of Contents

Indicates photo taken by Richard Michael Pruitt. All other photos taken by David Woo.

Owen Wilson

Actor, Writer

Pet: Garcia

I chose my pet's name because: The surfer Sunny Garcia. Although, most people think Jerry Garcia.

If I could change one thing about my pet, it would be: Nothing.

My pet's worst habit is: Can't think of one.

Behind my back people refer to me and my pet as: How would I know? Frick n' Frack because we're always together.

I wish my pet could: Travel everywhere with me. And, actually, he has been a lot of places.

Nobody knows my pet is: As young as he is. The breed, Blue Heelers, has grey hair in its coat and everyone assumes he's older.

My pet's best asset is: Loyalty.

If I had to choose a different pet, it would be: Besides a dog? This might be sacrilege in a book called *Top Dogs,* but I suppose a cat.

My pet's favorite treat is: Oddly enough, he likes avocados. Although, his favorite is marrow bone from the butcher.

My favorite time of the day to spend with my pet is: I like walking down to the ocean with Garcia in the morning.

Owen and Garcia

Jan Miller

CEO Dupree Miller & Associates

Pet: Schumacher

I chose my pet's name because: We named Schumacher after the famous F-1 Driver…my husband is a Ferrari freak!

If I could change one thing about my pet, it would be: That he would be nice to other dogs!

My pet's worst habit is: Being aggressive towards other male dogs.

Behind my back people refer to me and my pet as: Great shoppers. I love to shop and so does Schumacher. He's partial to Neiman Marcus, Scoop, Channel, and Louis Vuitton.

I wish my pet could: Talk! He howls when he wants something, but it would be great if he could speak English.

Nobody knows my pet: Has been written up in *F-1 Racing* magazine twice, and he has an autographed photograph of Michael Schumacher (the driver). It's signed "To Schu, From Schu."

My pet's best asset is: His bark. He has a great howl! Some people don't like a Beagle's relentless howling, but I love it!

If I had to choose a different pet, it would be: More Beagles!

My pet's favorite treat is: Chasing squirrels—he loves that more than food. He once had a squirrel treed for six hours. We finally made him come inside.

My favorite time of the day to spend with my pet is: At night, snuggling in bed.

Trisha Wilson

President/CEO, Wilson Associates
Pet: Charlie

I chose my pet's name because: I have always loved the name Charlie.

If I could change one thing about my pet, it would be: I wish I knew more about Charlie's first few months as a puppy. I found him when he was around nine months old. I never found out when his real birthday was so I decided to make it April 1.

My pet's worst habit is: Me. I spoil him just slightly!

Behind my back people refer to me and my pet as: People look at the two of us and say, "That's the biggest dog we have ever seen!"

I wish my pet could: I wish Charlie could travel with me everywhere I go. Because of his size, he, unfortunately, has to stay at home while I am away.

Nobody knows my pet is: A stray and doesn't have any Labrador in him, though he looks like a Labrador.

My pet's best asset is: His personality! He may seem intimidating and a bit scary, but he is a great big doll. I often find him greeting guests at the door with his orange, stuffed orangutan.

If I had to choose a different pet, it would be: I wouldn't. I have always loved dogs!

My pet's favorite treat is: His jumbo rawhide chews. Little does he know the natural chewing friction against his teeth helps to keep them clean.

My favorite time of the day to spend with my pet is: Saturday and Sunday mornings when we go on our walk together.

Chelsey "Sully" Sullenberger

Captain, US Airways
Pet: Twinkle

I chose my pet's name because: The name was chosen for us. She's a breeder dog for Guide Dogs for the Blind, and they are named at eight weeks old. Each litter is assigned a letter—she was part of the "T Litter." She didn't join us until she was eighteen weeks, so she was already Twinkle when she arrived.

If I could change one thing about my pet, it would be: The amount she sheds!

My pet's worst habit is: Her shedding.

Behind my back people refer to me and my pet as: Lorrie is crazy in love with Twinkle, so we're sure that people think she's too spoiled. She might be "just a dog" to them, but to us she's a member of the family.

I wish my pet could: …get well.

Nobody knows my pet is: …really an old lady with fur.

My pet's best asset is: She doesn't bark! She is also very obedient—extremely well trained.

If I had to choose a different pet, it would be: We'd love to have a Golden Retriever—in addition to Twinkle that is.

My pet's favorite treat is: Anything. She's a Lab after all.

My favorite time of the day to spend with my pet is: We go hiking every morning together—just saying the word "hike" is enough to get Twinkle excited!

Dr. Phil McGraw

Television Personality, Author
Pet: Maggie

I chose my pet's name because: We all chose Maggie's name together, but the driving force was my young son Jordan, who was eighteen at the time. He grew up as a real fan of the Simpsons television show, and for some reason was a big fan of "Maggie," the infant on the show. We decided to follow our practice of "loving an idea for fifteen minutes" to see how it felt. As soon as we started referring to her as Maggie, it just seemed that it was the only possible name to fit her. Her nickname is "Pup" and she responds to both. You would think with a career in psychology I would know better than to confuse a dog by giving her two different names!

If I could change one thing about my pet, it would be: Sometimes Maggie is too protective, and if a stranger moves too quickly when I'm in the room she really bristles up and shows her teeth. She has never bitten anyone, thank God.

My pet's worst habit is: See above.

Behind my back people refer to me and my pet as: He and that dog are inseparable. Maggie is a rescued dog that had been abandoned and won the "Doggie Lottery."

I wish my pet could: Go with me when I play golf and tennis. That's the only place I don't take her. She goes to work with me, travels with me here and abroad. She is so "jet set!"

Nobody knows my pet can: Stand flat footed and jump on top of an eight-foot fence. She is a jumper.

My pet's best asset is: A really expressive face. She can say more with an expression than a lot of people who can talk.

If I had to choose a different pet, it would be: A clone of Maggie.

My pet's favorite treat is: Riding in the car and hanging her head out the window. She has to have both back windows open so she can go back and forth constantly. I'll probably need a new back seat pretty soon.

My favorite time of the day to spend with my pet is: At night. She curls up by my feet in front of the fire. She is an "inspirational" sleeper!

Laura Bush

Former First Lady
Pets: Barney and Miss Beazley

I chose my pets' names because: Barney: He just looked like a Barney. Miss Beazley is named for the dinosaur in Oliver Butterworth's book, *The Enormous Egg.*

If I could change one thing about my pets, it would be: Barney and Miss Beazley often bring the mud and dirt inside after playing in the gardens.

My pets' worst habits are: Barney and Miss Beazley like to play "hard to get" with guests. Miss Beazley also likes to steal Barney's toys. When Miss Beazley demands to be let into the Oval Office, no matter who is meeting with the President.

Behind my back people refer to me and my pets as: "Don't they look alike?"

I wish my pets could: Hold up their end of the conversation.

Nobody knows my pets are: Barney thinks he is in training to be a Secret Service agent. He practices by standing very still next to the agent on duty and scanning all the activity. They are also good listeners. I sometimes practice my speeches with them.

My pets' best assets are: Barney is very handsome and a great athlete. He loves soccer — he can actually play soccer with his nose. Miss Beazley is an excellent tap dancer. The President always appreciates Barney and Miss Beazley's help on the golf course. They stick their noses in the hole and retrieve the balls when he sinks a putt.

If I had to choose a different pet, it would be: A horse.

My pets' favorite treats are: Barney loves to visit offices in the White House and see if any staff members have treats for him. Miss Beazley's favorite food is carrots—she thinks they are dog bones! Barney and Miss Beazley also like to visit the White House pastry shop for sweet treats.

My favorite time of the day to spend with my pets is: My favorite time of the day to spend with Barney and Miss Beazley is first thing in the morning. They always greet the day with enthusiasm and expect the best. I also enjoy spending time with them at the end of a long day; they help me unwind. I love seeing Barney run to greet the President at the end of the workday.

Laura Bush

Barney   *Miss Beazley*

Cesar Millan

Dog Behavior Expert
Pet: Daddy

I chose my pet's name because: He was already given the name! Many people don't know that Daddy originally belonged to rapper Redman. When the pit bull was four months old, Redman didn't feel he could care for it properly in his environment. He sought a trainer and, through a referral, found me. Daddy has been with the Millan family ever since!

If I could change one thing about my pet, it would be: Nothing! To me, Daddy is the perfect dog. He is calm, balanced, and a wonderful ambassador for his often misunderstood breed.

My pet's worst habit is: None. Because I took Daddy in so young, he never had a major issue, but in the beginning he was a little insecure. Since he had been moved around so much—Los Angeles, New Jersey, then back to L. A.—this was to be expected, but even that insecurity went away really fast.

Behind my back people refer to me and my pet as: Cesar and Daddy.

I wish my pet could: Live forever. I am grateful for every moment I have with him.

Nobody knows my pet is: My guru. Daddy knows me better than my mom, my kids, my therapist, even my wife!

My pet's best asset is: He always knows what to do in any scenario. Daddy has never made a mistake—never, never. He's never displayed aggression or any other negative behavior. He's just always helped me. Now he's passing that legacy on to his new student, Junior.

If I had to choose a different pet, it would be? None.

My pet's favorite treat is: A cow knee bone.

My favorite time of the day to spend with my pet is? All day.

Steve Miller

Recording Artist, The Space Cowboy,
The Gangster of Love, The Joker, Maurice
Pets: Lady, Daisy, and Maisey

I chose my pets' names because: My wife chose them.

If I could change one thing about my pets, it would be: Nothing.

My pets' worst habits are: Waking up early.

Behind my back people refer to me and my pets as: The luckiest dogs and human they know.

I wish my pets could: Talk.

Nobody knows my pets are: Boss.

My pets' best assets are: Their hearts.

If I had to choose a different pet, it would be: A horse.

My pets' favorite treats are: Two-inch thick Porterhouse steaks.

My favorite time of the day to spend with my pets is? Just before going to sleep.

Steve Miller
Lady . Daisy & Maisey

Diane Rehm

Executive Host & Producer/*The Diane Rehm Show*
WAMU/NPR
Pet: Maximillian (Maxie)

I chose my pet's name because: He's a long-haired Chihuahua, and Maximillian (Maxie for short) seemed a good choice.

If I could change one thing about my pet, it would be: Absolutely nothing!

My pet's worst habit is: Barking when my next-door neighbor comes to her door.

Behind my back people refer to me and my pet as: Nutsy.

I wish my pet could: Talk.

Nobody knows my pet is: …as funny as he is.

My pet's best asset is: He's perfectly loving.

If I had to choose a different pet, it would be: Don't wanna think about it.

My pet's favorite treat is: Small pieces of my meatloaf.

My favorite time of the day to spend with my pet is: Bedtime.

Diane A. Rehm
and
MAXIE

Ty Murray

Seven-Time World Champion All-Around Cowboy

Pet: Grey

I chose my pet's name because: Because he is grey and I like one-syllable names.

If I could change one thing about my pet, it would be: He is sixteen years old and I would like to make him two years old.

My pet's worst habit is: Nothing, he is perfect in his nature. I think bad pet habits come from humans.

Behind my back people refer to me and my pet as: ?????

I wish my pet could: Fly.

Nobody knows my pet: Follows direction at liberty and bridles.

My pet's best asset is: His horsenality.

If I had to choose a different pet, it would be: I love all animals, and I think elephants are awesome.

My pet's favorite treat is: Tender grass.

My favorite time of the day to spend with my pet is: Mornings and evenings.

Joe Cocker

Recording Artist

Pet: Ben

I chose my pet's name because: Actually, that was his name when we adopted him.

If I could change one thing about my pet, it would be: His fear of lightening and thunderstorms.

My pet's worst habit is: Gazing and silently begging for food. He's always looking for an unexpected treat.

Behind my back people refer to me and my pet as: Quite the pair. Or possibly "the nappers," since we both enjoy our Colorado siesta time.

I wish my pet could: Stay on the trail. On occasions Ben has selective hearing and a mind of his own no doubt.

Nobody knows my pet is: Most do not know that Ben snores.

My pet's best asset is: Being friendly.

If I had to choose a different pet, it would be: A cat.

My pet's favorite treat is: Food of any kind, if allowed, but he definitely loves his doggy treats.

My favorite time of the day to spend with my pet is: Anytime of the day really. I especially look forward in coming home off tour to see Ben. We're always happy to return to our daily routine of long hikes and spending time in the greenhouse.

Joe Cocker
&
Ben

Jerry Jeff Walker

Recording Artist
Pets: Coco and Jolie

I chose my pets' names because: They are actually my wife's dogs—I adopted them. Coco, because my wife got her in Paris, and Jolie is Cajun.

If I could change one thing about my pets, it would be: Their sibling rivalry.

My pets' worst habits are: They want to ride on my lap in the car.

Behind my back people refer to me and my pets as: No one has the nerve to tell me.

I wish my pets could: Drive themselves to the groomer.

Nobody knows my pets are: Tattooed on the inside of her ear, it's a registration in France.

My pets' best assets are: Their undying love.

If I had to choose a different pet, it would be: A parrot.

My pets' favorite treats are: Beggin' Strips.

My favorite time of the day to spend with my pets is: Nighttime.

Jerry Jeff Walker
Coco + Jolie

Ashley Force Hood

Professional Race Car Driver
Pet: Simba

I chose my pet's names because: He looks like a lion, so we named him after Simba from *The Lion King*. We originally named him Clutch Dust, which is what I'm covered with when I climb out of my race car after a pass, but it was too hard to say when I'd call him down for dinner, so we changed it to Simba!

If I could change one thing about my pet, it would be: We love to take him to the races and he absolutely loves staying in my race lounge and hotels with us. Unfortunately he tends to get car sick if the drive is very bumpy. If anyone's ever driven on the I5 freeway (which is pretty much our road out of town), they understand our problem!

My pet's worst habit is: He's very lovable…at about 4:30 a.m! He literally snuggles and rubs his face all over mine and has even stuck his nose up my nostril! It is impossible to sleep through that, much less breathe, so whether I like it or not, I am now a morning person.

Behind my back people refer to me and my pet as: Pathetically close….he's like my kid! My new husband, Dan, and I went on our honeymoon over New Year's and I missed my cat terribly! It was then that Dan made me pinky swear that he and the cat would at least get equal attention from me. I've only had Simba for a few months so he can't complain!

I wish my pet could: Talk. Doesn't everyone?

Nobody knows my pet is: He is actually a stellar athlete. He can do back flips and skid sideways through a room like you wouldn't believe, and that's not even with catnip!

My pet's best asset is: He's got a very lovable and playful personality. Also, his fur is the softest fur I've ever felt and people always comment on it. My father is horribly allergic to animals and basically anything with fuzz or feathers and yet my cat doesn't bother him at all! It's a miracle.

If I had to choose a different pet, it would be: I wouldn't trade Simba for anything but I would love to add a puppy to the mix some day! With our travel schedules this will have to wait though.

My pet's favorite treat is: This is not a treat that we will give him again, but by accident we discovered that he loves Kahlua and Cream! On the night before Christmas, as my family all sat around the tree opening each other's gifts, we weren't paying attention and figured the cat was playing in the wrapping. When we hadn't heard him in a few minutes, we turned around and there he was with his head in my drink! We grabbed the cup from him but by then he was already tipsy! (Just kidding.)

My favorite time of the day to spend with my pet is: Even though he drives me crazy, I love how lovable he is in the early morning. He's still a baby, so I worry that someday he'll grow out of it, so I make sure not to take any nose in the nostril moments for granted!

Ashley Force Hood
"Simba"

Nigel Marven

Wildlife Host

Pet: White Snake

I chose my pet's name because: I named him after the rock band, even though all snakes are deaf.

If I could change one thing about my pet, it would be: A rat snake can live for twenty years or more; I wish he'd live forever.

My pet's worst habit is: Sometimes he sheds his skin in pieces so I have to dampen the patches still attached and pull them off with forceps.

Behind my back people refer to me and my pet as: How would I know—it's behind my back!

I wish my pet could: Talk to me.

Nobody knows my pet is: A boy, but here's a tip—female snakes have shorter tails than male ones.

My pet's best asset is: He is so easy to keep. All he needs to thrive is a thawed out rat every week or so (I keep them in a special freezer), clean water, the right temperature (seventy-five to eighty-five degrees) and a secure hiding place.

If I had to choose a different pet, it would be: Mandarin rat snakes from China are really beautiful.

My pet's favorite treat is: A freshly killed rat, instead of a thawed out frozen one.

My favorite time of the day to spend with my pet is: Any time.

Nigel Marven
"White Snake"

Isaac Mizrahi

Fashion Designer
Pet: Harry

I chose my pet's name because: I chose the name Harry because it's HAPPY with "R"s instead of "P"s. Also, it is close to the word HAIRY, which Harry is very.

If I could change one thing about my pet, it would be: Harry has intimacy issues. He doesn't like to cuddle, which of course makes me love him even more, weirdly. But, I do wish he would cuddle once in awhile.

My pet's worst habit is: When he's nervous, he bites his paws.

Behind my back people refer to me and my pet as: Behind my back, I'm sure people call me Harry's bitch. I know other dogs do.

I wish my pet could: I wish Harry could talk. We communicate beautifully without words, but it would be wonderful every now and then, if he could bid at the bridge table without the bridge box.

Nobody knows my pet is: No one knows Harry is Jewish.

My pet's best asset is: His comic timing.

If I had to choose a different pet, it would be: There couldn't possibly be a different pet.

My pet's favorite treat is: Harry loves the Chicken Yakitori from Japonica Restaurant.

My favorite time of the day to spend with my pet is: I love very cold afternoons in Greenwich Village when we have free time to walk and walk.

Isaac Mizrahi & Harry

Pat Green

Singer/Songwriter
Pet: Moose

I chose my pet's name because: Isn't it obvious???

If I could change one thing about my pet, it would be: He's so needy…just kidding—nothing.

My pet's worst habit is: Poop.

Behind my back people refer to me and my pet as: A little ridiculous.

I wish my pet could: Make some money.

Nobody knows my pet is: More famous than I am.

My pet's best asset is: Home security.

If I had to choose a different pet, it would be: A real moose.

My pet's favorite treat is: No such thing…he eats what we do.

My favorite time of the day to spend with my pet is: When we snuggle… I've completely lost my masculinity.

Shirley Jones

Motion Picture and Television Icon, Oscar Winning Actress

Pet: Buff

I chose my pet's name because: My husband hated it.

If I could change one thing about my pet, it would be: That his breed's life-expectancy was longer.

My pet's worst habit is: He "LOVES" EEEEVERRYYbody (mainly criminals, vagrants, and methane addicts).

Behind my back people refer to me and my pet as: A mixed marriage.

I wish my pet could: Speak.

Nobody knows my pet is: Jewish.

My pet's best asset is: He "LOVES" EEEEVERRYYbody.

If I had to choose a different pet, it would be: A Great Dane.

My pet's favorite treat is: I tried them all. They taste awful.

My favorite time of the day to spend with my pet is: Homecoming.

Shirley Jones

&

Buff

Mike Modano

NHL All-Time U.S.-Born Points Leader, Dallas Stars Center

Pet: Bear

I chose my pet's name because: He's named after Jack Nicklaus, the golfer's nickname, "Golden Bear."

If I could change one thing about my pet, it would be: He could dry himself off after the twenty times a day he's in the pool!

My pet's worst habit is: Fly-by bitings! When he's playing hard with a toy or dog sometimes, he's so excited, he'll bite your ankle or butt!

Behind my back people refer to me and my pet as: Father and son.

I wish my pet could: Talk to me.

Nobody knows my pet is: Also a shredder.

My pet's best asset is: His speed.

If I had to choose a different pet, it would be: An elephant.

My pet's favorite treat is: Apples.

My favorite time of the day to spend with my pet is: Early mornings outside swimming.

Mike Modano
&
Bear

Robert Wagner

Actor, Author, Max's Human

Pet: Max

I chose my pet's name because: We name most of our pets after actors. We named him Max for Lionel Stander in *Hart to Hart,* who was our dear friend.

If I could change one thing about my pet, it would be: That he would live as long as we do.

My pet's worst habit is: Jumping up on us and not coming when he's called, but he is young.

Behind my back people refer to me and my pet as: That I am Max's dog.

I wish my pet could: Talk.

Nobody knows my pet is: Trilingual—Spanish, English, and German.

My pet's best asset is: His loyalty

If I had to choose a different pet, it would be: I refuse to choose.

My pet's favorite treat is: To ride in the car—he loves it!!

My favorite time of the day to spend with my pet is: Morning, noon, and night.

Mack Brown

Head Coach of the Texas Longhorns, National Champions
Pets: Charlie and Crockett

I chose my pets' names because: Crockett—Davy Crockett came from Tennessee to Texas. Charlie—Charlie Brown is Sally Brown's brother.

If I could change one thing about my pets, it would be: Not a thing. They are characters, but in a great way.

My pets' worst habits are: Eat too much.

Behind my back people refer to me and my pets as: Dogs are too big.

I wish my pets could: Lose some weight.

Nobody knows my pets are: Cavalier King Charles.

My pets' best assets are: So friendly.

If I had to choose a different pet, it would be: Yellow Lab

My pets' favorite treats are: They love all treats.

My favorite time of the day to spend with my pets is: At home at night.

Mack Brown

Crockett

Charlie

Lisa Loeb

Grammy Award-Winning Singer/Songwriter

Pet: Chinchy Morty

I chose my pet's name because: Chinchy Morty. He's soft like a chinchilla and it was the first name that came to me.

If I could change one thing about my pet, it would be: I wish his nails wouldn't grow.

My pet's worst habit is: Biting.

Behind my back people refer to me and my pet as: Lisa and that crazy cat.

I wish my pet could: Go outside to play, but it's not that safe in Los Angeles, with the cars and the coyotes.

Nobody knows my pet is: A robot sometimes.

My pet's best asset is: His cuteness.

If I had to choose a different pet, it would be: A clone of my cat Chinchy.

My pet's favorite treat is: He likes to play with strawberries, but he actually eats dried shrimp treats.

My favorite time of the day to spend with my pet is: In the morning when I wake up, he needs some petting, and often he sits on my lap, trying to get my attention while I'm on the computer.

Lisa Loeb

+ Chinchy Morty

Jay McGraw

Creator and Executive Producer of Daytime #1 New Show, *The Doctors*

Pet: Bizant

I chose my pet's name because: He already knew his name when we got him. Yes, my cat knows his name. And it enhances his Russian roots.

If I could change one thing about my pet, it would be: I would love to see what he could do with opposable thumbs.

My pet's worst habit is: He likes to wake me up too early in the morning.

Behind my back people refer to me and my pet as: How am I supposed to know that? They say it behind my back!

I wish my pet could: Talk. I would love to know why he does the things he does.

Nobody knows my pet is: Required to wear sunscreen when in the sun.

My pet's best asset is: Well, he's so beautiful, of course!

If I had to choose a different pet, it would be: A Bulldog.

My pet's favorite treat is: He loves cottage cheese and chocolate ice cream. Seriously!

My favorite time of the day to spend with my pet is: At night, before Erica and I go to bed.

Jay McGraw
& Bizant

Ron White

Comedian

Pets: Gurdie and Pearl

I chose my pets' names because: These names got up and picked these dogs themselves.

If I could change one thing about my pets, it would be: They would be fire-engine red.

My pets' worst habits are: Liking others more than me.

Behind my back people refer to me and my pets as: Timmy and Rin Tin Tin.

I wish my pets could: Sing.

Nobody knows my pets are: Made from wheat.

My pets' best assets are: 401K.

If I had to choose a different pet, it would be: Cardboard.

My pets' favorite treats are: Eggs Benedict.

My favorite time of the day to spend with my pets is: Mourning or anytime someone dies.

Roger Staubach

Hall of Fame Quarterback

Pet: Ryan

I chose my pet's name because: After Father Joe Ryan—great Catholic Chaplain and friend.

If I could change one thing about my pet, it would be: She has arthritic joints.

My pet's worst habit is: Snoring some nights—sleeps in her bed in our room.

Behind my back people refer to me and my pet as: The quarterback and he is the receiver.

I wish my pet could: Fetch the newspaper.

Nobody knows my pet: Likes to go to Starbucks with me and I get him pumpkin bread.

My pet's best asset is: Kindness to everyone including the grandkids.

If I had to choose a different pet, it would be: I would get another Lab.

My pet's favorite treat is: Milk Bones and pumpkin bread.

My favorite time of the day to spend with my pet is: Night—she is glad when I get home.

Willa Ford

Actress/Singer

Pets: Scout, Bella, and Bear

I chose my pets' names because: Actually, they were already named when I became their Mommy!

If I could change one thing about my pets, it would be: STOP SHEDDING!

My pets' worst habits are: Scout—pretends he doesn't understand me, but he does! Bella—hogging the bed. Bear—running around with my underwear.

Behind my back people refer to me and my pets as: Blondes.

I wish my pets could: Use the toilet! Live longer!

Nobody knows my pets are: Scout—a great speller. Bella—a therapist. Bear —a pain in my butt! But we love him!

My pets' best assets are: The genuine friendship and affection they give.

If I had to choose a different pet, it would be: A monkey.

My pets' favorite treats are: Corn on the cob (just the cob).

My favorite time of the day to spend with my pets is: Nighttime, snuggled up on couch!

Willa

Scout   Bella   Lil' Bear

B. J. Thomas

Recording Artist

Pets: Sophia, Scooter, and LuLu

I chose my pets' names because: Of what I can see of the dogs' character and because of the sound of the names.

If I could change one thing about my pets, it would be: Well, they are all very stubborn, but that's the way dogs are, I suppose.

My pets' worst habits are: You know, pooping in the house.

Behind my back people refer to me and my pets as: B. J. and the "spawns of Satan."

I wish my pets could: I wish that all my dogs could live forever.

Nobody knows my pets are: As mean as snakes.

My pets' best assets are: Their faithfulness.

If I had to choose a different pet, it would be: A pot-bellied pig.

My pets' favorite treats are: Any kind of meat or something extra.

My favorite time of the day to spend with my pets is: In the morning with my coffee; at night watching TV; and, of course, I love to sleep with them.

Sophia, Scooter & LuLu

Cristina Ferrare

Talk Show Host, *New York Times* Best-Selling Author

Pets: Cher, Axl Rose, Bella

I chose my pets' names because: My girls Alex and Arianna did; Cher (Poodle) is after well... Cher; Axl Rose (Chihuahua) is after another rock star; and Bella (Maltese), just because.

If I could change one thing about my pets, it would be: To stop using the carpet in the living room as one giant wee wee pad!!

My pets' worst habits are: Barking when the doorbell rings. With all three going at the same time, it's not fun!!

Behind my back people refer to me and my pets as: You mean people talk about me behind my back?

I wish my pets could: Massage my feet!

Nobody knows my pets are: Cujo when left alone too long, which is hardly ever, so I don't get it!

My pets' best assets are: Their backside! It stays small no matter how much they eat!!

If I had to choose a different pet, it would be: I wouldn't.

My pets' favorite treats are: Bacon.

My favorite time of the day to spend with my pets is: At night watching TV and having a cup of tea. Cher and Bella are on each side of me and Axl is under my shirt asleep.

Jimmy Johnson

Sports Analyst/FOX Sports

Pet: Buttercup

I chose my pet's name because: My wife Rhonda liked it for her "girl."

If I could change one thing about my pet, it would be: Nothing!

My pet's worst habit is: Waking up every day at 5 a.m. or 2 a.m. when we are in L.A.

Behind my back people refer to me and my pet as: Strange combination.

I wish my pet could: Live forever.

Nobody knows my pet is: Pampered like she is.

My pet's best asset is: Friendliness.

If I had to choose a different pet, it would be: No pet.

My pet's favorite treat is: Any people food.

My favorite time of the day to spend with my pet is: Evening.

Jimmy Johnson

Buttercup

Bob "Daddy-O" Wade

Artist

Pet: Lone Star

I chose my pet's name because: He reminds me of my forty-foot Iguana sculpture that was on the roof of the Lone Star Café in New York City.

If I could change one thing about my pet, it would be: Those sharp toe nails.

My pet's worst habit is: Hanging on to my bald head.

Behind my back people refer to me and my pet as: One Bearded Dragon was enough.

I wish my pet could: Bark.

Nobody knows my pet is: A party reptile.

My pet's best asset is: Hanging in there.

If I had to choose a different pet, it would be: A Southern Black Mouth Cur.

My pet's favorite treat is: Banana splits with flies.

My favorite time of the day to spend with my pet is: When he's awake.

Bob "Daddy-O" Wade

Carly Patterson

2004 Olympic All-Around Gymnastics Champion

Pet: Beijing

I chose my pet's name because: I chose to name my cat Beijing because I had just returned from an international meet in China. My mom said I could get a cat when I got home. She was all black with green eyes and I wanted to name her in memory of my trip.

If I could change one thing about my pet, it would be: I wish my cat didn't shed so much.

My pet's worst habit is: My pet doesn't have any bad habits. She is the sweetest!

Behind my back people refer to me and my pet as: People say my cat is a cat-dog because she is very loving and not as aloof as most cats.

I wish my pet could: I wish Beijing could talk and tell me what she needs when she meows.

Nobody knows my pet is: From Kittyco Rescue Center.

My pet's best asset is: Beijing has the most beautiful big green eyes (same color as mine).

If I had to choose a different pet, it would be: I also have a dog named Dolce.

My pet's favorite treat is: Beijing loves when I treat her to a little bit of milk.

My favorite time of the day to spend with my pet is: I love to spend anytime with my cat when I'm home.

Andrew Solomon

Author, Winner of the National Book Award, Pulitzer Prize Finalist,
and Lecturer in Psychiatry at Weill Cornell Medical College

Pet: River

I chose my pet's name because: He came with his name, which was a great relief, as I'd have named him something far more pretentious and it wouldn't have suited him as well to go through life as Prince Andrei Bolkonsky or Gabriel Garcia Lorca.

If I could change one thing about my pet, it would be: If I'm thinking in terms of his best interests, which I guess I would, I'd alleviate the arthritis that has dawned in later life. If I were being purely selfish, I'd like him to urinate all at one time and in one place.

My pet's worst habit is: Eating sticks on country afternoons and then vomiting woodchips, copiously, a few hours short of dawn.

Behind my back people refer to me and my pet as: They refer to him as the best thing about me.

I wish my pet could: Live forever.

Nobody knows my pet is: As completely and utterly delightful as he is entirely by nature and that none of it is any reflection on me or on the way my husband and I have brought him up.

My pet's best asset is: To be constantly interested in life, and to find in routines that are, if one is to be entirely honest, somewhat repetitive, an exuberant plenty of thrilling novelty and an eternally sufficient joy.

If I had to choose a different pet, it would be: If I had to choose an *additional* pet, it would be the phoenix, for sheer novelty value and because I am fond of mythology, but if I had to choose a *different* pet, I'd cry.

My pet's favorite treat is: Fond though he is of table scraps, much as he loves his Greenies (see picture in outtakes), exuberant though he is about exercise, what he really likes is our undivided focus. I live for art; he lives for love.

My favorite time of the day to spend with my pet is: Our waking and sleeping hours coincide somewhat imperfectly, as he is a morning animal and I am a night owl, but I'd say our mutual favorite time to be together is after dinner, when I respond to e-mail and he gets his evening treat and flops down in my study to ponder my continuing weird preoccupation with doing things other than play with him.

James Baker

Attorney, Politician, Political Administrator, and Political Advisor

Pet: Josh

I chose my pet's name because: He already had his name when I got him.

If I could change one thing about my pet, it would be: Nothing.

My pet's worst habit is: Dropping his first few bites of food on the floor. He is a finicky eater.

Behind my back people refer to me and my pet as: Joined at the hip.

I wish my pet could: Talk.

Nobody knows my pet is: Perfect.

My pet's best asset is: His nose. He is a fabulous retriever.

If I had to choose a different pet, it would be: His clone.

My pet's favorite treat is: Steak.

My favorite time of the day to spend with my pet is: Anytime we are hunting together.

James A. Baker III
&
Josh

Anne Marion

Business Executive/Owner of the 6666 Ranch in Texas

Pet: Kelly

I chose my pet's name because: Kelly was named after my lawyer and because it is an Irish name. He is originally an Irish farm dog.

If I could change one thing about my pet, it would be? Make him younger.

My pet's worst habit is: Jumping.

Behind my back people refer to me and my pet as: EARS aren't in the back of my head.

I wish my pet could: Bring me the newspaper.

Nobody knows my pet is: A Soft-Coated Wheaten Terrier.

My pet's best asset is: Disposition.

If I had to choose a different pet, it would be: A monkey.

My pet's favorite treat is: Cheese and turkey.

My favorite time of the day to spend with my pet is: The mornings when I read the papers.

Anne Marion and Kelly

George H. W. Bush

Former President George Herbert Walker Bush, "Gampy"

Pet: Sadie

I chose my pet's name because: We chose our pet's name, Sadie, because she was given to us by our dear friends, Sarah and Will Farish. Sarah's nickname is "Sadie."

If I could change one thing about my pet, it would be: No change.

My pet's worst habit was: Sadie had no bad habits, until she got a lot older, and then she was dragging.

Behind my back people referred to me and my pet as: I have no idea.

I wish my pet could: I can think of nothing Sadie could have done differently. She was the perfect pet.

Nobody knows my pet is: In "heaven."

My pet's best asset was: Sadie was kind and loving.

If I had to choose a different pet, it would be: When Sadie passed away, we got a new little fluff ball named Bebe. She is a Maltipoo.

My pet's favorite treat was: Getting her biscuits at night.

My favorite time of the day to spend with my pet was: All day long.

Nolan Ryan

Hall of Famer and President of the Texas Rangers

Pet: Lela

I chose my pet's name because: My mother's name was Martha Lee, but everyone called her "Lela."

If I could change one thing about my pet, it would be: That she would listen better to my commands. She likes to run off and "hunt" anything that flies.

My pet's worst habit is: Her puppy habit of chewing things.

Behind my back people refer to me and my pet as: A dog lover.

I wish my pet could: Bathe herself.

Nobody knows my pet is: Already good at pointing birds.

My pet's best asset is: Covering a lot of ground in a short period of time.

If I had to choose a different pet, it would be: A yellow Lab.

My pet's favorite treat is: Nolan Ryan tender-aged beef.

My favorite time of the day to spend with my pet is? Late afternoons when we go walking and/or running.

Dean Fearing

Chef/Partner of Fearing's Restaurant

Pet: Gumbo

I chose my pet's name because: It's food related.

If I could change one thing about my pet, it would be: He didn't poop in the tub.

My pet's worst habit is: He poops in the tub.

Behind my back people refer to me and my pet as: Two peas in a pod.

I wish my pet could: Talk.

Nobody knows my pet is: The best cat in the world!

My pet's best asset is: Kindness and friendliness.

If I had to choose a different pet, it would be: A dog.

My pet's favorite treat is: Petting.

My favorite time of the day to spend with my pet is: Morning.

Rosson Crow

Artist

Pet: Willie

I chose my pet's name because: Willie is named after Willie Nelson! He is one of my favorite country singers. Someday I want to get another Shih-Tzu named Waylon.

If I could change one thing about my pet, it would be: Nothing—he's perfect!

My pet's worst habit is: Stealing all the attention!

Behind my back people refer to me and my pet as: Ridiculous!

I wish my pet could: Speak with a French accent.

Nobody knows my pet is: My best friend.

My pet's best asset is: His hair…and his ability to defy gender stereotypes!

If I had to choose a different pet, it would be: A horse!

My pet's favorite treat is: A room full of people waiting to give him attention.

My favorite time of the day to spend with my pet is: All day…Willie loves hanging out at the studio with me.

Greg Biffle

NASCAR Sprint Cup Driver

Pet: Foster

I chose my pet's name because: I thought of a bunch of names. My favorite two were Max and Foster. I just liked Foster the best.

If I could change one thing about my pet, it would be: His lifespan. I wish it was the same as mine.

My pet's worst habit is: He snores.

Behind my back people refer to me and my pet as: They say we are inseparable.

I wish my pet could: I wish Foster could talk.

Nobody knows my pet is: ?????

My pet's best asset is: His personality. He can open and close doors. He learns new things quickly, even though he is eight years old.

If I had to choose a different pet, it would be: I wouldn't.

My pet's favorite treat is: He loves 3M's Dental Bones.

My favorite time of the day to spend with my pet is: Anytime is a great time to spend with Foster.

"Foster"

Alan Bean

First Artist to Paint Another World and
Fourth Man to Walk on the Moon
Pets: Fudgie and Puff

I chose my pets' names because: Fudgie was named in honor of a dog that we loved very much. We chose the name Puff because she is extra soft and gentle and has been since she was a tiny puppy.

If I could change one thing about my pets, it would be: That they would live as long as we do.

My pets' worst habits are: They don't seem to have bad habits.

Behind my back people refer to me and my pets as: He is completely nutty about those two dogs.

I wish my pets could: Talk and tell me what they are thinking, especially when they don't feel good.

Nobody knows my pets are: Better friends than most any human, especially when I make a mistake.

My pets' best assets are: Their ability to forgive and forget.

If I had to choose a different pet, it would be? More Lhasa Apso littermates!

My pets' favorite treats are: They love "BunnyBites," which are treats that Leslie (my wife) makes and names in honor of Fudgie and Puff's sister, Bunny Bunbumpers.

My favorite time of the day to spend with my pets is: Nap time, when Fudgie is nestled next to me and Puff is snoring softly in my ear.

Juliet Huddy

Co-Host of the Nationally Syndicated Morning Show,
The Morning Show with Mike and Juliet
Pet: Gomez

I chose my pet's name because: Gomez is a Chihuahua, which is a town in Mexico. My original name for him was Nugget. I had that for a day, but then I was sitting at lunch with my good friend Rebecca Gomez, and something just hit me. I asked her if she would be offended if I named him Gomez, and she not only said she wasn't offended, she said she loved it! But another reason is that Gomez was the name an old friend of mine called my dad. She said he looked like Gomez Adams, the dad in the *Adams Family*. She was totally right.

If I could change one thing about my pet, it would be: His inability to understand that bath mats and rugs are not pee pee pads.

My pet's worst habit is: He likes to, how shall I say this politely, show off his manhood—all the time.

Behind my back people refer to me and my pet as: Party animals.

I wish my pet could: Dance on his own without me having to move him around. I love to sing KC and the Sunshine Band's "Get Down to Night" and make him do his sexy dog dance. It's absolutely hilarious. At least it is to my fiancé and me.

Nobody knows my pet is: A descendant of Russian aristocracy (canine, not human).

My pet's best asset is: His big bug eyes.

If I had to choose a different pet, it would be? I WOULD NEVER! But, if I HAD to, I'd choose a monkey.

My pet's favorite treat is: The vegetables in his hard food. He likes to take each of them out, one at a time, bring them over to a private location, feast on them, then repeat.

My favorite time of the day to spend with my pet is: When I'm watching TV with my fiancé and he cuddles in between us.

Juliet
&
Gomez

Travis Brorsen

Winner of *Greatest American Dog* on CBS

Pet: Presley

I chose my pet's name because: My roommate at the time was a musician and I thought if he helped name him, he would take on some of the responsibility. Well, being fans of Elvis, we gave him the name of Presley. Unfortunately, he never helped pick up the poop!

If I could change one thing about my pet, it would be: I would love for Presley to realize that laying beside me is just as good as laying on me.

My pet's worst habit is: Gas. He can clear a room with the best of them.

Behind my back people refer to me and my pet as: Newlyweds.

I wish my pet could: Understand me when he's standing in front of the TV and I'm trying to change the channel! He just hasn't learned, "GET OUT OF THE WAY!"

Nobody knows my pet is: Embarrassed when people watch him go potty.

My pet's best asset is: Presley's best asset is his love for people and children. He would play 24/7 if I didn't make him take a break.

If I had to choose a different pet, it would be: Another boxer…they're the best companions and, of course, Presley could use a girlfriend.

My pet's favorite treat is: Hot dogs…he loves hot dogs.

My favorite time of the day to spend with my pet is: I love spending time with Presley at the park. Boxers love to burn off energy by running in giant circles. Presley looks like a race horse at least four times a week.

Daryl Richardson

Director/Founder of The Dallas World Aquarium

Pets: Maya and Andy

I chose my pets' names because: Maya's arrival coincided with the opening of the "Mundo Maya" exhibit. Andy was Audrey, until the DNA came back!

If I could change one thing about my pets, it would be: They both are exactly what they are supposed to be.

My pets' worst habits are: Maya sleeps late; Andy loves to bite your buttons!

Behind my back people refer to me and my pets as: My alter egos!

I wish my pets could: Be cloned.

Nobody knows my pets are: Ready to run or fly off with the next stranger.

My pets' best assets are: Maya's tail wagging and Andy's beautiful wings.

If I had to choose a different pet, it would be: Not necessary!

My pets' favorite treats are: Beef Tenderloin for both, raw for Andy and grilled for Maya.

My favorite time of the day to spend with my pets is: During the day with Andy, when he basks outside the office; with Maya, when I arrive home, she acts like I have been gone for months!

MAYA AND ANDY

Kellie Rasberry

Co-Host of the Nationally Syndicated *Kidd Kraddick in the Morning* Show

Pet: George

I chose my pet's name because: My brother is two years younger than I am and when he was just a toddler, whenever anybody would ask him "Ryan, what's your name?" he would say, "George!"—SO cute. And after taking just one look at my Yorkie-Poo Poo, I knew I'd found my own cute little George.

If I could change one thing about my pet, it would be: I love him dearly, but whenever anybody walks their dog in front of our house he goes CRAZY NUTS. I can walk him on a leash and we'll pass dogs and squirrels and people and cars, and he stares straight ahead without flinching. But, if somebody DARES to walk past the front of our house, the barking is deafening.

My pet's worst habit is: Licking. He loves to lick people's legs, feet and hands. Believe it or not, some people find that to be quite disgusting.

Behind my back people refer to me and my pet as: I don't know! It's behind my back!

I wish my pet could: Do a "Stupid Pet Trick" so we could get a free trip to NYC and I could meet David Letterman.

Nobody knows my pet is: What got me through my divorce. While everyone was praising me for my bravery, he was the one I cried to and held onto every night.

My pet's best asset is: His face. It's like looking into the face of a little boy.

If I had to choose a different pet, it would be: I don't know why anybody would have anything other than a Yorkie-Poo Poo!

My pet's favorite treat is: Beggin' Strips. He gets one every morning when I walk out the door for work.

My favorite time of the day to spend with my pet is: Bedtime. He sleeps curled up to me every night.

XO
Kellie Rasberry
and
George!

Dr. Alfred Gilman

Nobel Laureate, Chief Scientific Officer of the Cancer Prevention
and Research Institute of Texas

Pet: Boo

I chose my pet's name because: She came with her (I think dumb) name; we should have changed it.

If I could change one thing about my pet, it would be: Her name…see above.

My pet's worst habit is: Assuming all who visit have come soley to play with her.

Behind my back people refer to me and my pet as: No comment.

I wish my pet could: Predict world economic disasters and stock market crashes.

Nobody knows my pet is: No comment.

My pet's best asset is: Her owners; especially her "Mom."

If I had to choose a different pet, it would be: No comment.

My pet's favorite treat is: A week's vacation with her dog sitter, who speaks her language!

My favorite time of the day to spend with my pet is: No comment.

Pat Summerall

Legendary Sports Broadcaster
Pet: Miss Gracie (Amazing Grace)

I chose my pet's name because: *Amazing Grace* is the name of our home, so we named her Amazing Grace and call her Miss Gracie.

If I could change one thing about my pet, it would be: She would like to swim in the pool.

My pet's worst habit is: Begging.

Behind my back people refer to me and my pet as: Spoiled.

I wish my pet could: Talk.

Nobody knows my pet is: Going to day care.

My pet's best asset is: She loves unconditionally.

If I had to choose a different pet, it would be: Another Lab.

My pet's favorite treat is: When I sneak her french fries.

My favorite time of the day to spend with my pet is? Early morning.

Pat Summerall and Miss Gracie

Sara Hickman

Mother/Musician/Creator Elf

Pet: Mimi

I chose my pet's name because: She told me to call her that!

If I could change one thing about my pet, it would be: That she could live forever!

My pet's worst habit is: Swiping your leg as you pass by—with claws extended—when she wants some attention.

Behind my back people refer to me and my pet as: Venus and Serena!

I wish my pet could: Drive—or control government spending.

Nobody knows my pet is: A Harvard graduate in Marine Biology.

My pet's best asset is: Her breath. It does not stink!

If I had to choose a different pet, it would be: This is a silly question! My other beloved family pets are Jeff Goldblum (snake), Lucky (our Jack Russell) and eighteen fish.

My pet's favorite treat is: A trip to the spa!

My favorite time of the day to spend with my pet is: Right now.

Herb Kelleher

Founder and Chairman Emeritus, Southwest Airlines

Pet: Susie

I chose my pet's name because: My wife, Joan, who rescued abandoned Susie from a public park, announced her name without prior consultation with me. That is also how our four children were named!

If I could change one thing about my pet, it would be: I would bring her back to life (beloved Susie died in the fall of 2008).

My pet's worst habit was: Attacking my daughter Julie's dog, Sheila—the ONLY dog she didn't get along with. They must have had a serious disagreement.

Behind my back people referred to me and my pet as: "Smarmy" or "Kissy-Kissy."

I wish my pet could: Retrieve, instead of hiding with her ball and making you find her and wrestle it away.

Nobody knows my pet was: Eighteen years old.

My pet's best asset was: Her affectionate intelligence.

If I had to choose a different pet, it would be: None.

My pet's favorite treat was: Frozen steak bones.

My favorite time of the day to spend with my pet was: The evening, after work.

Herb Kelleher
&
Susie

Jack Graham

Pastor

Pets: Deuce and Yogi

I chose my pets' names because: Deuce was named after our first beagle, Nike. His registered name is Nike II. Yogi was named after baseball great Yogi Berra.

If I could change one thing about my pets, it would be: We are still training our boys to not jump on people. Needless to say, we have a ways to go.

My pets' worst habits are: To my wife's horror…killing rabbits!

Behind my back people refer to me and my pets as: Most people are very complimentary about the beagle boys to my face, so I don't have any idea about what else is being said behind my back.

I wish my pets could: Sleep in our bedroom…however, we are not to that point yet!

Nobody knows my pets are: Spoiled rotten.

My pets' best assets are: They are loving, and show it freely.

If I had to choose a different pet, it would be: I think I would have a Sheltie. We had one once and he was a great dog.

My pets' favorite treats are: Bacon.

My favorite time of the day to spend with my pets is: Hanging out with the boys and watching the Mavericks and Rangers. They are big fans.

Sandra Brown

New York Times Best-Selling Author
Pets: Lucky and Chase

I chose my pets' names because: They were named after the brothers in my Texas trilogy, Chase and Lucky.

If I could change one thing about my pets, it would be: Their fear of thunderstorms.

My pets worst habits are: Licking, "hot spots."

Behind my back people refer to me and my pets as: Having matching hairdos.

I wish my pets could: Talk.

Nobody knows my pets are: Fraidy cats.

My pets' best assets are: Sweet, docile personalities and tolerance of grandsons.

If I had to choose a different pet, it would be: Another Golden Retriever.

My pets' favorite treats are: Left over steak and scrambled eggs.

My favorite time of the day to spend with my pets is: Late evening.

Dr. Denton Cooley

Founder and President of the Texas Heart Institute

Pet: Belle

I chose my pet's name because: She was a beauty (Belle). Pick of the litter.

If I could change one thing about my pet, it would be: She wants me to throw her the ball to fetch—too often.

My pet's worst habit is: Sleeping on the sofa.

Behind my back people refer to me and my pet as: "Gruesome Twosome"

I wish my pet could: Talk.

Nobody knows my pet is: Super intelligent.

My pet's best asset is: She is safe with little children.

If I had to choose a different pet, it would be: A Dachshund.

My pet's favorite treat is: An ice cream cone.

My favorite time of the day to spend with my pet is: Evening.

Denton A. Cooley MD

and

Belle —

Charlie Waters

Former Dallas Cowboy
Pet: Jackson

I chose my pet's name because: I needed a name that is not related phonetically with any training words, like no, or heel, or stay, so no "Joe" or "Steel" or "Grey." I also like a "hard," one-syllable name that is not the name of a family member, to avoid association. So Jackson, turned into "Jack," when training him.

If I could change one thing about my pet, it would be: I'd fix his broken tail, as it has been damaged somehow, and is always tucked over towards his left side.

My pet's worst habit is: He will jump in the water quicker than a hiccup when I am not paying attention. Nasty, stagnant, muddy water.

Behind my back people refer to me and my pet as: That person who lives for his dogs.

I wish my pet could: Live healthy for as long as I do.

Nobody knows my pet is: Quite tough and not afraid of anything.

My pet's best asset is: His awareness and consideration for me.

If I had to choose a different pet, it would be: "Kind of species" pet it would be? A cat.

My pet's favorite treat is: Play ball with me all the time for the rest of his life. Favorite food treat is peanut butter.

My favorite time of the day to spend with my pet is: Saturday afternoon.

Charlie Waters
+
Jackson

Catherine Crier

Broadcast Journalist, Attorney, and Partner of Cajole Entertainment

Pets: Digger, Bella, Dixie Chick, Sam, Abbey, and
Boomer (the black dog, passed away in August, 2008)

I chose my pets' names because: They fit!

If I could change one thing about my pets, it would be: Nothing.

My pets' worst habits are: The big guys: none. The little ones: occasionally missing the "pads" in the house.

Behind my back people refer to me and my pets as: Who knows?

I wish my pets could: Live as long as I plan to.

Nobody knows my pets are: Angels returned to earth.

My pets' best assets are: Mind reading.

If I had to choose a different pet, it would be: Another dog (I have four horses).

My pets' favorite treats are: Whatever I'm eating.

My favorite time of the day to spend with my pets is: All the time; but I love the "waking up love attacks" by the two Yorkies—snuggle time before I get out of bed.

Cath
Bella, Boomer, Digger, Chicken, Sam & Abbey

Amen Wardy

Retailer

Pets: Casady, Fancy, Freckles, and Katie

I chose my pets' name because: Casady (name of creek which flows thru the ranch), Fancy (came named), Freckles (obvious), Katie (named after a previous dog I loved).

If I could change one thing about my pets, it would be: I would love to know what they are thinking.

My pets' worst habits are: Bringing me presents (i.e. dead chipmunks and mice, deer legs, etc.).

Behind my back people refer to me and my pets as: Mutt & Jeff.

I wish my pets could: Live forever!

Nobody knows my pets are: My best friends!

My pets' best assets are: Unconditional love.

If I had to choose a different pet, it would be: A pink pig.

My pets' favorite treats are: Dried salmon!

My favorite time of the day to spend with my pets is: In the mornings when we take the first walk.

Amen Wardy
Casady, Fancy,
Freckles, & Katie

Robert Decherd

Chairman of the Board, President and CEO of A. H. Belo Corporation

Pet: Charlie

I chose my pet's name because: My daughter suggested it.

If I could change one thing about my pet, it would be: Her extreme sensitivity to changes in barometric pressure (i.e., thunderstorms).

My pet's worst habit is: Destroying dog crates and selected woodwork.

Behind my back people refer to me and my pet as: Hopeless.

I wish my pet could: Talk.

Nobody knows my pet is: Neurotic.

My pet's best asset is: Her protective instinct.

If I had to choose a different pet, it would be: A Wheaten Terrier.

My pet's favorite treat is: Rawhide chews.

My favorite time of the day to spend with my pet is: Early morning.

Robert Decherd
& Charlie

George W. Bush

Forty-Third President of the United States

Pet: Barney

If I could change one thing about my pet, it would be: Be friendlier to others.

My pet's worst habit is: Ignoring people.

Behind my back people refer to me and my pet as: Co-dependent.

I wish my pets could: Feed himself.

Nobody knows my pet: Likes to fish.

If I had to choose a different pet, it would be: A cat.

My pet's favorite treat is: Meat.

My favorite time of the day to spend with my pet is: Evening.

George Bush

BARNEY

Boone Pickens

CEO, BP Capital

Pet: Murdock

I chose my pet's name because: I thought it was an interesting name for a dog and it wasn't common.

If I could change one thing about my pet, it would be: He would be two instead of twelve.

My pet's worst habit is: His expectations are too high for his master.

Behind my back people refer to me and my pet as: Boone and his assistant.

I wish my pet could: Talk.

Nobody knows my pet is: He snores!

My pet's best asset is: He loves everybody!

If I had to choose a different pet, it would be: Another dog.

My pet's favorite treat is: Strawberries.

My favorite time of the day to spend with my pet is: Before bed.

Boone Pickens
&
Murdock

Karen Hughes

Public Relations/Communications Executive,
Global Vice Chairman of Burson-Marsteller
Pet: Breeze

I chose my pet's name because: My husband and son are huge sports fans, so all our animals are named after sports figures. When we got our puppy in the fall of 1999, the local high school quarterback was Drew Brees (now the quarterback for the New Orleans Saints). "Breeze" is an adaptation of his name.

If I could change one thing about my pet, it would be: She's the best dog I've ever had and has an affectionate, enthusiastic personality so I don't think I would change anything.

My pet's worst habit is: Being too rambunctiously friendly when we have dinner guests, especially if they don't like dogs as much as we do!

Behind my back people refer to me and my pet as: How would I know if it's behind my back? My husband says I talk to everyone like I talk to my dog…of course, I love my dog.

I wish my pet could: Live as long as I do.

Nobody knows my pet is: Afraid to walk through half-open doors.

My pet's best asset is: Her devoted, enthusiastic personality.

If I had to choose a different pet, it would be: Another Golden Retriever.

My pet's favorite treat is: A big stuffed animal that she can tear up and drag around.

My favorite time of the day to spend with my pet is: Our neighborhood walks together. She gets excited when we take out our tennis shoes, and we can't use the word "walk" unless we are going to take one because she knows what it means!

Karen Hughes

Breeze

Larry Mahan

Rodeo Six-Time All-Around World Champion and
Two-Time World Champion Bull Rider

Pet: Ms.

I chose my pet's name because: Ms., after the magazine, *Ms.* I thought it was a good magazine that gave women a chance to express themselves for things they were concerned about.

If I could change one thing about my pet, it would be: I'd like for her to be younger. She has a cow sense and loves to work cattle.

My pet's worst habit is: No bad habits!

Behind my back people refer to me and my pet as: What a smart dog! She really communicates well and understands.

I wish my pet could: Live longer than me.

Nobody knows my pet: Helps me understand unconditional love.

My pet's best asset is: Me.

If I had to choose a different pet, it would be: Same dog.

My pet's favorite treat is: For me to compliment her, tell her she did a good job and that she makes me happy.

My favorite time of the day to spend with my pet is: All the time. I let her run loose around all the animals.

Larry Mahan
Be Boppin' Bob
Ms.

Fess Parker

Actor/Real Estate Developer/Vintner

Pet: Tuxedo

I chose my pet's name because: He was already named when we got him.

If I could change one thing about my pet, it would be: I would like for him to have a few more good years of life.

My pet's worst habit is: Barking uncontrollably when I have visitors ring the bell at my home.

Behind my back people refer to me and my pet as: Honestly, I'm not sure.

I wish my pet could: Do tricks, any kind.

Nobody knows my pet is: Very sneaky.

My pet's best asset is: Marcella and I can take him to our Inn and even with the noise of the people laughing and singing, he is so well-behaved.

If I had to choose a different pet, it would be: Another Standard Poodle.

My pet's favorite treat is: Chicken strips and Greenies. He waits for them every night.

My favorite time of the day to spend with my pet is: In the evening when we are watching TV, he wants our complete attention and to snuggle.

Fess and Tuxedo Parker

Colleen Barrett

President Emeritus, Southwest Airlines
Pets: Button (right) and Blubber (left)

I chose my pets' names because: Button because he is cute as a button. Blubber because he was an American Eskimo and dogs eat whale blubber in Alaska, I thought "Blubber" would be an appropriate name.

If I could change one thing about my pets, it would be: Button: I would make him want to eat the special diet that his vet put him on because it is good for him—he hates his special food and gets very mad at me when I won't give him the "good" (from his perspective) stuff! Blubber: I would bring back his sharp hearing and superb eyesight.

My pets' worst habits are: Button: He jumps high when going after food and his spine is out of alignment as a result thereof; he also jumps on me because he is so excited to see me and he always hits a soft spot in my leg that causes me agonizing pain every time he does it. Blubber: He ate paper and/or towels, washcloths, etc., and he dragged stuff under my dinning room table causing me have to get down under there and try to clean it up.

Behind my back people refer to me and my pets as: I have no idea.

I wish my pets could: I wish Button could remember things longer than one minute and I wish he would not "scold" me (by barking at the top of his lungs) when he knows I am late with his dinner. I wish Blubber could have talked.

Nobody knows my pets are: Button: Not really a puppy (I always call him the puppy because he is younger than his older brother, who passed on Father's Day of 2009)—he is actually 14 years old which certainly doesn't qualify as a puppy. Blubber: My best friend—he kept all my secrets!

My pets' best assets are: Button: He is always happy; he is always lively; if he were a human being, he would always be whistling—he's always optimistic. Blubber: He had a beautiful and intelligent smile; he was a great watchdog when he was younger—I always knew when a storm was coming before I ever heard thunder and if someone drove into my driveway before they even got to the doorbell, he would be at the door barking to welcome them.

If I had to choose a different pet, it would be: None.

My pets' favorite treats are: Button: Hot dogs or M&Ms. Blubber: Hot dogs.

My favorite time of the day to spend with my pets is: Button: Early morning when I am swimming and he is "guarding" the backyard. Blubber: Nighttime, especially after a long, difficult day.

Luv,
Colleen Barrett

Tony Dorsett

Legendary Running Back
Pet: Charlie

I chose my pet's name because: Charlie is the name of the girls' maternal grandfather.

If I could change one thing about my pet, it would be: He wouldn't bark soooo much!

My pet's worst habit is: Chewing on the shutters.

Behind my back people refer to me and my pet as: TD and his boy.

I wish my pet could: Let himself out to go potty.

Nobody knows my pet is: One of my best buddies.

My pet's best asset is: Cute as a button.

If I had to choose a different pet, it would be: A panther.

My pet's favorite treat is: Bacon.

My favorite time of the day to spend with my pet is: At night, watching ESPN.

Byron Nelson

Golf Legend

Pet: Peppy Lee Bueno

I chose my pet's name because: That's the name he came with and it refers to some well-known Quarter-Horse bloodlines.

If I could change one thing about my pet, it would be: Sure wish I could ride him myself—I bought him for my wife, Peggy.

My pet's worst habit is: Doesn't come to you unless you have treats — gourmet horse cookies!

I wish my pet could: Play golf. Just think how far he could kick a golf ball.

Nobody knows my pet is: A golfer at heart.

My pet's best asset is: He's kind. When I first saw him, I told Peggy that Peppy has kind eyes.

If I had to choose a different pet, it would be: Probably a Collie dog.

My pet's favorite treat is: Gourmet horse treats—we call them "cookies"—and Peppy sure does know that word.

My favorite time of the day to spend with my pet is: Whenever Peggy rides Peppy, she brings him to me when I'm in the shop so I can say hello.

Dr. Andrew Ordon

Plastic Surgeon Icon and Host of *The Doctors*

Pet: Lulu

I chose my pet's name because: My family thought it would be rather ironic or funny to give her a cute girly name despite her less-than-feminine appearance.

If I could change one thing about my pet, it would be: She could smell a bit better.

My pet's worst habit is: That has to be a tie between farting and snorting.

Behind my back people refer to me and my pet as: Beauty and the Beast. You can choose who is who.

I wish my pet could: Clean up after herself!

Nobody knows my pet is: Actually, quite fast…when put to the test.

My pet's best asset is: She is a lover, tried and true.

If I had to choose a different pet, it would be: It could be fun to try the French version and go for a French Bulldog.

My pet's favorite treat is: Pig ears, hands down.

My favorite time of the day to spend with my pet is: Mid-day nap time is the best, she's a bit dopey and very lovey.

Ashley Paige

Animal Advocate/Cruelty Free Fashion Designs

Pets: Tri-pod and Petunia

I chose my pets' names because: I don't—I let the new owners do that.

If I could change one thing about my pets, it would be: They would have never been abused.

My pets' worst habits are: Peeing where everyone else does.

Behind my back people refer to me and my pets as: The dog lady who makes bikinis.

I wish my pets could: Fly.

Nobody knows my pets are: Allowed to run the house!

My pets' best assets are: Always changing—always a new foster dog.

If I had to choose a different pet, it would be: Horses—they are just like dogs.

My pets' favorite treats are: Steak—I'm veggie, so they rarely get it.

My favorite time of the day to spend with my pets is: I wish—I am a Foster Mommy to them. It's a full time job.

Ashley Paige

Petunia

Tri-Pod

W. Herbert Hunt

Advisor to Management, PetroHunt LLC.

Pets: Sweet Pea, Bitsy, and Miss Daisy

I chose my pets' names because: I live with them for about a month before the name is a final fix. Left to right: Sweet Pea—started as Sweetie, but since I like sweet peas it quickly became Sweet Pea. Bitsy—started as Little Bits, but has been shortened to Bitsy. Miss Daisy—quickly determined she had a mind of her own, so she was named Miss Daisy from the movie *Driving Miss Daisy*.

If I could change one thing about my pets, it would be: Get them to wait until 6 a.m. to wake us up.

My pets' worst habits are: Saying hello by barking at joggers and people walking their dogs as they go by.

Behind my back people refer to me and my pets as: Being nutty about each other.

I wish my pets could: Mind my wife better.

Nobody knows my pets are: Smarter than I am.

My pets' best assets are: Being so cute that they are "Chick Magnets." When out walking, women always stop us to cuddle them.

If I had to choose a different pet, it would be: I couldn't. We are strictly "Yorkie" people.

My pets' favorite treats are: Anything we are eating. They have a bench seat at the table.

My favorite time of the day to spend with my pets is: We enjoy watching TV together and especially like Cesar Millan's show *The Dog Whisperer* as they bark and growl at the dogs, cows, horses, and some men actors with gruff voices.

Art work of three dogs by Nancy Hunt

Lou Dobbs

CNN Anchor and Host of *Lou Dobbs Tonight*
Pet: Rocky

I chose my pet's name because: Rocky Road Ice Cream is a family favorite!

If I could change one thing about my pet, it would be: Not a single thing.

My pet's worst habit is: A slight tendency to drool.

Behind my back people refer to me and my pet as: "A little large."

I wish my pet could: Remember he is not a lap dog!

Nobody knows my pet is: Imported.

My pet's best asset is: A bright, happy nature—he shares with everyone!

If I had to choose a different pet, it would be: An elephant.

My pet's favorite treat is: Anything from the dinner table.

My favorite time of the day to spend with my pet is: Mornings.

Lou Dobbs
Rocky

Hugh Aynesworth

Author/Journalist

Pet: Bugsy

I chose my pet's name because: We discovered her in our garage about ten years ago…happily terrorizing bugs!

If I could change one thing about my pet, it would be: Make her a newborn to be able to enjoy her longer.

My pet's worst habit is: Bugsy really likes to talk…LOUDLY…when she wants something.

Behind my back people refer to me and my pet as: Cat Daddy.

I wish my pet could: Understand that newspapers are to read, not to sprawl on.

Nobody knows my pet is: The most loving pet I've ever had.

My pet's best asset is: Her love and trust.

If I had to choose a different pet, it would be: A Koala Bear…?

My pet's favorite treat is: Four meals a day.

My favorite time of the day to spend with my pet is: In the morning when she joins us in bed.

Hugh Aynesworth
&
Bugsy

Nancy Lieberman

Basketball Hall of Famer and ESPN Broadcaster/Commentator

Pets: Nemo and Link

I chose my pets' names because: It was original. Nobody else on the block had them.

If I could change one thing about my pets, it would be: That they could swim faster than Michael Phelps!

My pets' worst habits are: Can't come out and play.

Behind my back people refer to me and my pets as: Inseparable.

I wish my pets could: Watch Sports Center.

Nobody knows my pets are: Far-sighted.

My pets' best assets are: They are quiet and kind.

If I had to choose a different pet, it would be: A dog.

My pets' favorite treats are: Goldfish food.

My favorite time of the day to spend with my pets is: Checking on them in the morning to make sure they are alive.

Nancy Lieberman ☺

Nemo & Link

Phil Romano

Entrepreneur
Pet: P. J.

I chose my pet's name because: It is my initials.

If I could change one thing about my pet, it would be: Make him stop shedding.

My pet's worst habit is: Farting.

Behind my back people refer to me and my pet as: Looking alike; same color eyes.

I wish my pet could: Talk.

Nobody knows my pet is: Afraid of the water.

My pet's best asset is: His loving nature.

If I had to choose a different pet, it would be: A Playboy Bunny.

My pet's favorite treat is: Leftovers from Eatsi's and Nick & Sam's!

My favorite time of the day to spend with my pet is: Walking after dinner.

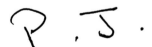

Joe Camp

Creator of the Canine Superstar Benji,
Director/Writer of All Five of the *Benji* Movies;
Author of the Best-Seller, *The Soul of a Horse:*
Life Lessons from the Herd
Pet: Benji

I chose my pet's name because: There's an entire book about that. The name Benji actually came from a Yorkshire Terrier that we owned when the story for the original *Benji* movie was being written. His full name was Sir Benjamin of Courtney but he was never called anything but Benji. That Yorkshire Terrier was who taught me that dogs do talk, with their eyes. And that's where the dialog for the movie came from. From Benji's eyes.

If I could change one thing about my pet, it would be: Absolutely nothing.

My pet's worst habit is: Digging for gophers, usually right after a rain. Methinks she doesn't realize that she is supposed to act like a movie star.

Behind my back people refer to me and my pet as: Completely bonded.

I wish my pet could: Live forever.

Nobody knows my pet is: Don't know how to answer this one. Because of her popularity, folks pretty much know everything about her.

My pet's best asset is: Her big, beautiful brown eyes that tell everyone about the kind of pet they can find at their local animal adoption center.

If I had to choose a different pet, it would be: At the moment, I wouldn't.

My pet's favorite treat is: Food, literally any kind.

My favorite time of the day to spend with my pet is: She's always with me, pretty much around the clock. She's sleeping at my feet as I type this.

Tom Hicks

Sports Teams Owner

Pet: Ranger

I chose my pet's name because: Ranger is named after my baseball team, the Texas Rangers.

If I could change one thing about my pet, it would be: I wish he was five years younger.

My pet's worst habit is: Eating food off the counter.

Behind my back people refer to me and my pet as: I feed him too many treats.

I wish my pet could: Pick up dead quail better.

Nobody knows my pet is: My favorite dog.

My pet's best asset is: Loyalty and affection.

If I had to choose a different pet, it would be: Another Lab.

My pet's favorite treat is: Eating off the dinner table.

My favorite time of the day to spend with my pet is: Morning coffee and newspapers.

Lynn Neary

NPR Correspondent
Pet: Jazz (short for Jasmine)

I chose my pet's name because: My daughter and I both like it. My husband went along with our choice.

If I could change one thing about my pet, it would be: I wish she was friendlier to other creatures—squirrels, cats, and dogs, as well.

My pet's worst habit is: Barking when strangers come to the door.

Behind my back people refer to me and my pet as: Maya's mom and Maya's dog.

I wish my pet could: Tell me what she really wants and thinks.

Nobody knows my pet is: So smart.

My pet's best asset is: She's so cute.

If I had to choose a different pet, it would be: I wouldn't.

My pet's favorite treat is: Pretty much anything but fruits and vegetables.

My favorite time of the day to spend with my pet is: When I come home from work and she greets me like a long lost friend.

Lynn Neary
+
JAZZ

Kinky Friedman

Writer, Musician, and Former Texas Governor Candidate

Pet: Alice

I chose my pet's name because: I am a control addict.

If I could change one thing about my pet, it would be: I'd like bigger pigs.

My pet's worst habit is: Talking politics.

Behind my back people refer to me and my pet as: Jewish.

I wish my pet could: Fly.

Nobody knows my pet is: A lesbian.

My pet's best asset is: A good lobbyist.

If I had to choose a different pet, it would be: Kosher.

My pet's favorite treat is: A BLT.

My favorite time of the day to spend with my pet is: Five times a day for Muslim calls to prayer.

Kinky Friedman

Alice

The Art Guys
Jack Massing

Artist

Pet: Apple

I chose my pet's name because: She had her name when my wife picked her out of the adoption pen at the S. P. C. A.

If you could change one thing about your pet, what would it be? Annual income.

My pet's worst habit is: Snoring.

Behind my back people refer to me and my pet as: Jack and Apple.

I wish my pet could: Talk.

Nobody knows my pet is: Spade.

My pet's best asset is: Love and devotion.

If I had to choose a different pet, it would be: A giraffe.

My pet's favorite treat is: Budweiser.

My favorite time of the day to spend with my pet is: Late evening when there is time to pet her and talk to her slowly so she understands.

Michael Galbreth

Artist

Pet: Annie

I chose my pet's name because: "Hitler" just didn't seem friendly enough.

If I could change one thing about my pet, it would be: Her Phylum.

My pet's worst habit is: Talking behind my back.

Behind my back people refer to me and my pet as: His pet talks behind his back.

I wish my pet could: For once, tell the truth.

Nobody knows my pet is: Lying.

My pet's best asset is: Her subprime mortgage…oops strike that.

If I had to choose a different pet, it would be: Something else.

My pet's favorite treat is: Twenty cash.

My favorite time of the day to spend with my pet is: Cocktail hour.

Don Nelson

NBA Head Coach Golden State Warriors

Pets: Lucky and Kawika

I chose my pets' names because: Both my wife and I are cancer survivors and we've been very lucky in our life.

If I could change one thing about my pets, it would be: Nothing. I love the little guys just the way they are.

My pets' worst habits are: Putting their noses—literally—where they shouldn't be.

Behind my back people refer to me and my pets as: "Me and my best friends."

I wish my pets could: Rebound.

Nobody knows my pets are: Great swimmers.

My pets' best assets are: Loyalty. They never leave me!

If I had to choose a different pet, it would be: Goldfish.

My pets' favorite treats are: Lucky Charms.

My favorite time of the day to spend with my pets is? In the evening when I'm watching an NBA game on TV and smoking a cigar.

Don Nelson
Kawika
Lucky

Bo Pilgrim

Senior Chairman/Co-Founder of Pilgrim's Pride

Pet: Queenie

I chose my pet's name because: She is a queen to me, and her name is Queenie.

If I could change one thing about my pet, it would be: She smells especially bad when wet with long hair.

My pet's worst habit is: Going swimming, coming out drenched, running to me, shaking water on me from head to toe.

Behind my back people refer to me and my pet as: Quiet and reserved.

I wish my pet could: Leave the yard rabbits alone, for they too have rights, but not according to my wife.

Nobody knows my pet is: Getting very old.

My pet's best asset is: Happy tail wagging.

If I had to choose a different pet, it would be: A short-haired dog with Queenie's love for me.

My pet's favorite treat is: Extra chicken on top of tasteless, dry dog food.

My favorite time of the day to spend with my pet is: Arriving home at the end of the day, she comes running.

Bo Pilgrim and Queenie

Hannah Storm

ESPN SportsCenter Anchor and President of the Hannah Storm Foundation

Pet: Buttons

I chose my pet's name because: My eight-year-old daughter chose my dog's name, Buttons, before he was even with us. She had bugged me for a dog for a few years, and I finally relented when my husband was out of town, covering the Athens Olympics.

If I could change one thing about my pet, it would be: I wish Buttons wouldn't bite men's heels when they come to my back door. He is a nipper!!… and a fierce barker AFTER they leave.

My pet's worst habit is: Chewing Dixie cups and licking the dishes in the dishwasher. Silly, they think its funny I have a little dog like a Bijon—people picture me with a Lab or bigger dog!

Behind my back people refer to me and my pet as: No nicknames!!!

I wish my pet could: Brush his own teeth!

Nobody knows my pet is: As sweet as he is.

My pet's best asset is: A good snuggler when watching sports on TV.

If I had to choose a different pet, it would be: Just a different kind of dog—a big chocolate Lab!

My pet's favorite treat is: Anything that is not dog food.

My favorite time of the day to spend with my pet is: In the afternoon when I come home from work, and he is so excited. Then he jumps in my lap and curls up with me on the couch!

Hannah Storm and Buttons

Barbara Bush

Former First Lady

Pet: Sadie

I chose my pet's name because: Sarah and Will Farish gave her to me. I named her "Sadie" after Sarah.

If I could change one thing about my pet, it would be: That she would have lived to be one hundred!

My pet's worst habit was: She was perfect.

Behind my back people referred to me and my pet as: Close.

I wish my pet could: Talk.

Nobody knows my pet was: A hater of cats.

My pet's best asset was: Her love — unconditional.

If I had to choose a different pet, it would be: Hard to say. I am also the mother of a Maltepoo. This puppy made Sadie seem young again.

My pet's favorite treat was: Dog biscuits.

My favorite time of the day to spend with my pet was: All day!

Barbara Bush and Sadie

Roger Horchow

Founder of the Horchow Collection/Broadway Musical Producer

Pet: Daisy

I chose my pet's name because: My wife liked the name.

If I could change one thing about my pet, it would be: She could have many more years of life.

My pet's worst habit is: Barking to go outside and then barking to come back in one minute later because she knows she will get a cookie.

Behind my back people refer to me and my pet as: The old man and his black Lab.

I wish my pet could: Talk (softly).

Nobody knows my pet is: Thirteen.

My pet's best asset is: Loyalty and gentleness with my five grandchildren.

If I had to choose a different pet, it would be: A tame monkey.

My pet's favorite treat is: Dog cookie.

My favorite time of the day to spend with my pet is? Early a.m.

Roger Horchow

Daisy

Pam Minick

Champion Cowgirl

Pet: Seven

I chose my pet's names because: Actually, Jessie, our Ranch Manager named him "Seven"— he said after a famous John Wayne movie. We have never figured out which movie. Must be an Eastwood movie?

If I could change one thing about my pet, it would be: That he wasn't stubborn as a mule.

My pet's worst habit is: Biting, playfully, but it hurts.

Behind my back people refer to me and my pet as: My cute little ass.

I wish my pet could: Pull a wagon, that would be fun.

Nobody knows my pet is: A mama's boy (he is in a pasture with his mother).

My pet's best asset is: His looks—who can resist those big ears and expressive eyes.

If I had to choose a different pet, it would be: He is one of many varieties at our ranch.

My pet's favorite treat is: Sweet grain.

My favorite time of the day to spend with my pet is: Evenings, at feeding time. His "bray" is so loud and comical; he lets you know he's hungry.

Howard Rachofsky

Art Collector

Pet: Princess

I chose my pet's name because: She looks royal!

If I could change one thing about my pet, it would be: Her barking!

My pet's worst habit is: Barking

Behind my back people refer to me and my pet as: Obsessed with each other.

I wish my pet could: Stop barking.

Nobody knows my pet is: Losing the hair on her tail.

My pet's best asset is: Her cute face.

If I had to choose a different pet, it would be: I would not choose a different pet.

My pet's favorite treat is: Almond butter.

My favorite time of the day to spend with my pet is: Nap time.

Howard Rachofsky
&
Princess

Steve Hartnett

Money Manager/Restaurateur

Pet: Brooke

I chose my pet's name because: "A brook runs through it"—our backyard that is.

If I could change one thing about my pet, it would be: Live longer.

My pet's worst habit is: Sometimes stubborn.

Behind my back people refer to me and my pet as: Soul mates (along with my wife).

I wish my pet could: Talk.

Nobody knows my pet is: From a different planet.

My pet's best asset is: Temperament.

If I had to choose a different pet, it would be: A clone.

My pet's favorite treat is: Red meat.

My favorite time of the day to spend with my pet is: Evening.

Steve Hartnett

Brooke

Jay Allison

Chairman and CEO of Comstock Resources, Inc.

Pet: Jar Jar a. k. a. "Duke"

I chose my pet's name because: He looks like Jar Jar Binks in *Star Wars*.

If I could change one thing about my pet, it would be: No barking at squirrels, please.

My pet's worst habit is: Chasing birds.

Behind my back people refer to me and my pet as: The Runners—because I am an ultra marathon runner and he runs nonstop always.

I wish my pet could: Read the Sports page to me and fetch the newspaper.

Nobody knows my pet: Can actually "smile" at me.

My pet's best asset is: He is ALWAYS happy.

If I had to choose a different pet, it would be: Another rescue dog.

My pet's favorite treat is: A bone that he buried in the flower bed or popsicles (Grape).

My favorite time of the day to spend with my pet is: In the evening— watching him run.

Kathy Whitworth

LPGA Legend, World Golf Hall of Fame

Pet: Lucky

I chose my pet's name because: Lucky was already Lucky when adopted from the Flower Mound Humane Society.

If I could change one thing about my pet, it would be: To come into my life sooner.

My pet's worst habit is: Barking at other dogs while riding in the car.

Behind my back people refer to me and my pet as: Velcro Buddies.

I wish my pet could: Go everywhere with me.

Nobody knows my pet is: Arthritic due to a broken leg as a puppy.

My pet's best asset is: Just being Lucky.

If I had to choose a different pet, it would be: Difficult for me. But, I would definitely adopt a dog in need.

My pet's favorite treat is: The treat being offered at the moment!

My favorite time of the day to spend with my pet is: Every moment I have — especially for first light, early morning walks in the pasture.

Kathy Whitworth

Lucky

Big Al Mack

Co-Host of the Nationally Syndicated Radio Show
Kidd Kradick in the Morning
Pet: Queso

I chose my pet's name because: My mom called and asked me if I wanted a dog. She told me that the owner was going to take the unwanted dogs to the pound. At the time, I was sitting on the beach in Mexico eating chips and queso.

If I could change one thing about my pet, it would be: I would curb her appetite for expensive clothes and shoes.

My pet's worst habit is: (See above), ha ha.

Behind my back people refer to me and my pet as: Exactly the same…expensive taste and no cash!

I wish my pet could: GET A JOB!

Nobody knows my pet is: GAY! SHE LOVES GIRLS!

My pet's best asset is: HER BUTT!

If I had to choose a different pet, it would be: HOOTERS GIRL!

My pet's favorite treat is: Ketel One Vodka and Seven.

My favorite time of the day to spend with my pet is? Jogging early Saturday mornings.

Big Al + Queso

Dr. Shirley Cothran Barret

Former Miss America, Author, and Public Speaker

Pets: Dixie and Jack

I chose my pets' names because: Dixie is a southern lady! She has a real air of gentility and has impeccable manners at her dog bowl! Naturally quiet and demure…the name was perfect! Jack's fearless and valiant attitude dubbed him the name "Jack Bauer!" Always on high alert for any kind of action, our Jack is up to the challenge!

If I could change one thing about my pets, it would be: Nothing! Dixie is "Mom's dog." She is faithful, gentle, fiercely protective, and a loyal friend. Jack is a barker. He barks at EVERYTHING!! Because we live in the country, his frequent barking is not a problem…but sometimes, we just want Jack to chill out!

My pets' worst habits are: Dixie—She's perfect!!! What can I say? Jack—Can unrelenting barking cause permanent damage?

Behind my back people refer to me and my pets as: Twiddle Dee and Twiddle Dum! We are constant companions. Dixie and Jack protect me from strangers, squirrels, and even the occasional coyote that may be lurking around our country house.

I wish my pets could: I always thought it would be cool for my dogs to sing along with me. Unlike most people, I know Dixie and Jack would appreciate my talent!

Nobody knows my pets are: Dixie—PERFECT!!!! Jack—has a vertical jump of forty-two inches!!!!

My pets' best assets are: Dixie: her gentle spirit and fierce loyalty. Jack: the ability to make people laugh at his antics!

If I had to choose a different pet, it would be: Cats! Their independent spirit cracks me up! The old saying that dogs have masters and cats have slaves is so true! They have an attitude of "to know me is to love me."

My pets' favorite treats are: Bacon. Dixie loves bacon bits. Jack loves whatever Dixie doesn't gobble down first!

My favorite time of the day to spend with my pets is: Early evening…they are less frisky and more willing to play at MY pace. My husband and I will get on our four-wheeler and go down to the pond, where the dogs LOVE to swim and play in the water. They are, after all, Labs!

Dr. Shirley Cothran Barret

Dixie & Dallas

Sharon Gault

Makeup Artist
Pet: Sandy

I chose my pet's name because: I chose my pet's name because the movie *Annie* had an orphaned dog named Sandy that was very loving much like my pet.

If I could change one thing about my pet, it would be: Nothing. Sandy greets me every time I come into the house. It is almost like Sandy is not a dog at all, but a mini person; from curling in my arms and snoring while she is sleeping, to the excitement she exudes while watching the movie *Bolt*. I feel that all living animals should be treated equally because they are all God's special creations.

My pet's worst habit is: If Sandy is guilty of any bad habits it would be that she snores like a freight train passing through a small, quiet Southern town at 3 a.m.

Behind my back people refer to me and my pet as: People refer to us as inseparable and the odd couple.

I wish my pet could: I only wish that Sandy could better communicate with me other than our own special language we have built through our Mother-doggie bond.

Nobody knows my pet is: No one knows the extent of how deep my pet's love is for me. She is hands-down my special lady.

My pet's best asset is: My pet's best asset is the way she can light up a room with her brilliant and happy energy shown by her toothy smile and wiggle of her butt/tail.

If I had to choose a different pet, it would be: Well, you see, I would choose Sandy, but she would be a slick black panther pouncing prey and protecting her mama.

My pet's favorite treat is: Sandy has quite a fit around any and all human food even if she finds its taste dissatisfying or makes her ill.

My favorite time of the day to spend with my pet is: My favorite time with Sandy is the little moments at the end of the day right before I pass out when it seems like the world's stress melts away as I fall asleep with her in my arms. Who needs a man when you have a cuddle buddy like Sandy!

Sharon Gault
Mama Make-up

Scout

Vernon Fisher

Artist

Pet: Sparky

I chose my pet's name because: Because he was so energetic as a kitten.

If I could change one thing about my pet, it would be: For him to live forever.

My pet's worst habit is: Lying across the newspaper I'm trying to read.

Behind my back people refer to me and my pet as: If it's behind my back, how would I know?

I wish my pet could: Stop making so many grammatical errors.

Nobody knows my pet is: I suspect a spy from another planet.

My pet's best asset is: He cheerfully pays up when he loses a bet.

If I had to choose a different pet, it would be: A Border Collie named Arizona.

My pet's favorite treat is: Uncle Julio's chicken fajitas.

My favorite time of the day to spend with my pet is: After work.

VERNON FISHER
&
SPARKY

Mary Grace Eubank

Children's Book Illustrator, Dog Devotee and GRANDMOTHER
Pet: Happy

I chose my pet's name because: Happy was born on my birthday, July 28, hence her name, Pinecrest Birthday Party. That got shortened to "Happy Birthday" which became "Happy Dog."

If I could change one thing about my pet, it would be: Happy does not hear well, but then neither do I. Calling her is not really an issue because she is usually velcrowed to me, but she might be missing some uplifting rock 'n roll. Even though we have developed our own subtle, effective two-way communication I would give her a greater power of perceiving sound.

My pet's worst habit is: Happy gets depressed when I leave and do not take her with me.

Behind my back people refer to me and my pet as: Since I have an absurd abundance of Cavaliers, I think people probably refer to me as "that crazy dog lady."

I wish my pet could: Live forever.

Nobody knows my pet is: Simple. Simple is good.

My pet's best asset is: Happy's best asset is her insane sense of devotion and appetite for affection…AND, she makes me laugh.

If I had to choose a different pet, it would be: Another Happy Dog.

My pet's favorite treat is: Happy's favorite treat would probably be "candy Kisses," but she will have to settle for plain 'ol "people puckers." She is watching her waistline.

My favorite time of the day to spend with my pet is: Snuggling into bed at night.

Mary Grace Eubank

Happy Dog

Zig Ziglar

Author and Motivational Teacher

Pet: Fastidious (Fastie)

I chose my pet's name because: Her overwhelming commitment to cleanliness in every area of her life, and felt that Fastidious was the appropriate name for her.

If I could change one thing about my pet, it would be: I would teach her to wait until I get out of bed before she starts barking — not when she sees me turn over in bed.

My pet's worst habit is: Barking when people are walking down the street in front of our house.

Behind my back people refer to me and my pet as: "That dog is spoiling him!"

I wish my pet could: Go to her doggie door, but pick up the paper on her way in.

Nobody knows my pet is: Left-handed, but she doesn't consider it a handicap.

My pet's best asset is: Her ability to persuade my wife to give her more food. She even claims that we are starving her—which is not true!

If I had to choose a different pet, it would be: Another Welsh Corgi.

My pet's favorite treat is: A little more meat on the menu and a lot more food on special occasions.

My favorite time of the day to spend with my pet is: Early in the mornings on my walks, when both of us are a little more energized than later in the day.

Zig Ziglar
&
Fastidious

Biographies & Outtakes

 Allison, Jay—PAGE 176: M. Jay Allison has been chief executive officer of Comstock Resources, Inc. (NYSE:CRK), since 1988 and is the former chairman of Bois d'Arc Energy, Inc., NYSE. Jay received B.B.A., M.S. and J.D. degrees from Baylor University, where he served on the Board of Regents for nine years. He currently serves as a director of Tidewater Marine, Inc. (NYSE:TDW); on the advisory board of the Salvation Army, and as chair of the board of trustees of Legacy Christian Academy in Frisco, Texas. Jay is the 2009 Energy Sector Ernst & Young Entrepreneur of the Year in the Southwest Region North. Jay runs ultramarathons as a hobby.

 Art Guys, The—PAGE 159: Michael Galbreth and Jack Massing are most well known for their public spectacles and staged performances which blur the line between life and art. Galbreth—born in Philadelphia in 1956—and Massing—born in Buffalo in 1959—began working together in 1983 while students at the University of Houston. The Art Guys use sculpture, drawing, video, performances, and installations to express their views and expand the boundaries of art. Their work has been included in more than 150 exhibitions in museums, galleries, and public spaces throughout the United States as well as Europe and China with more than forty solo exhibitions.

 Aynesworth, Hugh—PAGE 144: Hugh G. Aynesworth is a journalist who was born on August 2, 1931, in Clarksburg, West Virginia. He was the lead reporter for *The Dallas Morning News* at the time of the John F. Kennedy assassination and was the first print reporter to interview Lee Harvey Oswald's widow, Marina Oswald. He later became a true-crime author, co-writing the books *The Only Living Witness* and *Conversations with a Killer* about serial killer Ted Bundy. He later was a staff correspondent for *Newsweek* magazine and then a reporter for *The Washington Times.*

 Baker, James—PAGE 75: James Addison Baker III is a attorney, politician, political administrator, and political advisor. He was born on April 28, 1930, and graduated from Princeton University in 1952. He earned a J.D. in 1957 from The University of Texas at Austin and began to practice law in Texas. He served as the chief of staff in President Ronald Reagan's first administration and in the final year of the administration of President George H. W. Bush. Baker also served as secretary of the treasury from 1985–88 in the second Reagan administration, and secretary of state in the George H. W. Bush administration. He is also the namesake of the James A. Baker III Institute for Public Policy at Rice University in Houston, Texas. OUTTAKE**1**

 Barrett, Colleen—PAGE 131: Colleen C. Barrett is the president emeritus of Dallas-based Southwest Airlines. She is best known as the "heart of the airline" and largely responsible for the company's manic focus on delivering "Positively Outrageous Customer Service." She was born September 14, 1944, in Bellows Falls, Vermont, and is a highest honors graduate of Becker Junior College in Worcester, Massachusetts. Among her accolades, Colleen was bestowed the Horatio Alger Award in 2005; named one of the Outstanding Women in Aviation in 2007; was the recipient of the 2007 Tony Jannus Award; and was inducted into the Texas Labor Management Hall of Fame in 2008. She is widely recognized as one of America's leading businesswomen.

 Bean, Alan—PAGE 88: Alan LaVern Bean was born March 15, 1932, and is a former NASA astronaut. He became the fourth person to walk on the moon in November 1969 at the age of thirty-seven. Bean graduated from R. L. Paschal High School in Fort Worth, Texas. He received a Bachelor of Science degree in aeronautical engineering from the University of Texas at Austin in 1955. After a four-year tour as a fighter pilot assigned to a jet attack squadron in Jacksonville, Florida, he trained as a Navy test pilot where his instructor was his future Apollo 12 Commander Pete Conrad. He was awarded an honorary doctorate of science from Texas Wesleyan College in 1972, and presented an honorary doctorate of engineering science degree from the University of Akron in 1974.

 Biffle, Greg—PAGE 87: Gregory Jack Biffle was born December 23, 1969, in Vancouver, Washington. He is a NASCAR Sprint Cup Series driver who drives the #16 3M Ford Fusion for Roush Fenway Racing. Greg took the Rookie of the Year Award in the NASCAR Craftsman Truck Series in 1998 and the Rookie of the Year Award in the Busch Series in 2001. In 2002, Greg won his first NASCAR Sprint Cup Series race in July at Daytona. Greg and his wife, Nicole, manage a foundation to create awareness and serve as an advocate to improve the well-being of animals by engaging the power and passion of the motorsports industry. The foundation donates to local humane societies, no-kill animal shelters, spay and neuter clinics, and the Animal Adoption League. OUTTAKE**2**

 Brorsen, Travis—PAGE 92: Travis Brorsen and Presley are best known for competing in CBS's summer reality hit *Greatest American Dog.* They won top honors along with $250,000, the most ever won by a dog. He has guest starred on hit shows like *Desperate Housewives, Bones, JAG,* and *Over There,* just to name a few. Travis can be seen in dozens of national commercials for Kay Jewelers, Net Zero, Chevy, and currently running spots for Zales, Boeing, and Rooms To Go with Cindy Crawford.

 Brown, Mack—PAGE 51: William Mack Brown was born on August 27, 1951, and is head coach of The University of Texas at Austin Longhorn football team. Brown attended Vanderbilt University and later graduated from Florida State University in 1974. He received his graduate degree from The University of Southern Mississippi in 1976. Prior to coaching at Texas, Brown coached at Appalachian State, Tulane, and North Carolina. In 2005, the Longhorns won the Big 12 conference and went on to win the national championship. In 2006 Brown was awarded the Paul "Bear" Bryant Award for Coach of the Year and on November 27, 2008, he achieved his 200th career win, making him the first Texas coach to reach that mark. OUTTAKE**3** Mack Brown is joined by his wife, Sally, for a portrait with their dogs, Charlie and Crockett.

 Brown, Sandra—PAGE 108: Sandra Brown, born Sandra Lynn Cox on March 12, 1948, in Waco, Texas, and was raised in Fort Worth. Brown is a best-selling author of romantic novels and thriller suspense novels. Brown has also published works under the pen names of Rachel Ryan, Laura Jordan, and Erin St. Claire. Brown began writing in 1981 after her husband challenged her to write a novel. Since then Sandra has published sixty-five novels and had over fifty *New York Times* best-sellers. Notable achievements include American Business Women's Association's Distinguished Circle of Success, B'nai B'rith's Distinguished Literary Achievement Award, A.C. Greene Award, and Romance Writers of America's Lifetime Achievement Award.

Be The Person
Your Dog
Thinks You Are

Bush, Barbara—PAGE 167: Barbara Pierce Bush was born on June 8, 1925, and is the wife of George H. W. Bush, the forty-first president of the United States, and mother of George W. Bush, the forty-third president, and former Florida Governor Jeb Bush. She served as first lady of the United States from 1989 to 1993, while her husband was president. Previously she had served as second lady of the United States for eight years. As the wife of the vice president and then president, and continuing after leaving Washington, she supported the cause of universal literacy. She serves on the boards of AmeriCares and the Mayo Clinic, and heads the Barbara Bush Foundation for Family Literacy. OUTTAKE **4**

 Bush, George H. W.—PAGE 79: George Herbert Walker Bush was born in Milton, Massachusetts, on June 12, 1924, and enlisted at age eighteen in the armed forces. The youngest pilot in the Navy when he received his wings, he flew fifty-eight combat missions during World War II. Bush was flying over the Pacific and was shot down by Japanese antiaircraft fire and was rescued from the water by a U. S. submarine. He was awarded the Distinguished Flying Cross for bravery in action. He graduated from Yale in 1948 with a bachelor's degree in economics. Bush served as the forty-first president of the United States from 1989 to 1993. Bush held a variety of political positions prior to his presidency, including vice president of the United States in the administration of Ronald Reagan (1981–89) and director of Central Intelligence under Gerald R. Ford. OUTTAKE **5** President George H. W. Bush poses for a quick photo with photographer David Woo's son Jake.

 Bush, George W.—PAGE 120: George W. Bush was born on July 6, 1946, in New Haven, Connecticut, to Barbara and George H. W. Bush. He received a bachelor's degree in history from Yale University in 1968 and then served as a pilot in the Texas Air National Guard. President Bush received a Master of Business Administration from Harvard Business School in 1975. George W. Bush was the 43rd president of the United States. He was sworn into office on January 20, 2001, re-elected on November 2, 2004, and sworn in for a second term on January 20, 2005. Before his presidency, he served for six years as governor of the State of Texas.

 Bush, Laura—PAGE 23: Laura Lane Welch Bush was born on November 4, 1946, and is the wife of the forty-third president of the United States, George W. Bush, and was the first lady of the United States from January 20, 2001 to January 20, 2009. She graduated from Southern Methodist University in 1968 with a bachelor's degree in education and went on to receive a master's degree in Library Science at the University of Texas at Austin. She met George W. Bush in 1977, and they were married later that year. Laura has been recognized for her interests in education and literacy and established the annual National Book Festival in 2001 and has encouraged education on a worldwide scale.

 Camp, Joe—PAGE 151: Joe Camp was born April 20, 1939, in St. Louis, Missouri, and is a film writer, producer, director, author, and passionate speaker. He has written several books and is best known as the creator and director of the canine superstar Benji. Camp has written, produced, and directed seven theatrical motion pictures including all of the *Benji* movies and cumulatively grossed over $600 million in today's dollars, making him one of the most successful independent filmmakers of all time. OUTTAKE **6**

 Cocker, Joe—PAGE 32: John Robert "Joe" Cocker was born in England in May of 1944. He became a popular artist in the 1960s for his rocker/blues style. He hit No. 1 in the UK with his version of the Beatles' *A Little Help From My Friends*. His cover of the Box Top's hit *The Letter* was his first U.S. Top Ten hit. Cocker went on to record such hits as *You Are So Beautiful* and *Up Where You Belong*. OUTTAKE **7** Sue Green, Joe's assistant and PR person, helps with the dogs for the photo shoot.

 Cooley, Dr. Denton—PAGE 111: Denton Arthur Cooley was born August 22, 1920, and is a pioneering American heart surgeon known for performing the first successful heart transplant in the United States as well as the first clinical implantation of a totally artificial heart. Denton graduated in 1941 from The University of Texas, then began his medical education at The University of Texas Medical Branch, Galveston, and then went on to complete his medical degree and his surgical training at Johns Hopkins University School of Medicine. Cooley and his associates have performed more than 100,000 operations—more than any other group in the world.

 Cothran Barrett, Dr. Shirley—PAGE 183: Shirley Cothran Barret has an earned doctorate degree from Texas Woman's University and is a contributing author to various publications, as well as pursuing personal goals in creative writing. As a professional speaker, Shirley has been entertaining and energizing audiences with her transparent and humorous candor for over thirty-five years. Appearing in civic, educational, and inspirational arenas, Shirley uses her life experiences to motivate, encourage, and edify her listeners to examine their present and future destinies. Shirley and her husband since 1976, Richard Barret, live in Texas and are parents to four grown children.

 Crier, Catherine—PAGE 115: Catherine Jean Crier was born November 6, 1954, and is a television personality and a former district court judge. Crier graduated with a Bachelor of Arts in Political Science and International Affairs from The University of Texas at Austin. She received her Juris Doctor from Southern Methodist University Dedman School of Law. Catherine became the youngest elected state judge in Texas history at age thirty and served as a Texas State District Judge for the 162nd District Court in Dallas County. From 1989 to 2007, Crier was a television personality on CNN, ABC News, Fox News, and Court TV which included her own show, *Catherine Crier Live*, which ran for six years, ending in April 2007. Aside from her TV work, she has authored several nonfiction books.

 Crow, Rosson—PAGE 84: Rosson Crow is a painter born in Dallas, Texas, in 1982. She lives and works in Los Angeles. She received her BFA from the School of Visual Arts in New York in 2004 and her MFA from Yale in 2006. Crow has had solo exhibitions at Honor Fraser, Los Angeles, White Cube, London, Galerie Nathalie Obadia, Paris, and CANADA gallery, New York. In 2009, Crow had a Focus Exhibition at the Modern Art Museum of Fort Worth, Texas. OUTTAKE **8**

 Decherd, Robert—PAGE 119: Robert Decherd has served as Chief Executive Officer of A. H. Belo Corporation or Belo Corp. since 1987, and has spent his entire career with the company, which is the oldest continuously operated business in the State of Texas. Robert graduated cum laude in 1973 from Harvard College, where he was president of *The Harvard Crimson*. He graduated cum laude from St. Mark's School of Texas in 1969, and later became president of the school's Board of Trustees, a Distinguished Alumnus, and a Life Trustee. A. H. Belo owns four daily newspapers, with *The Dallas Morning News* being the flagship, and Belo Corp. is the nation's largest publicly-owned pure play television company, with twenty-one local television stations and three cable news channels in some of the country's largest markets. Robert has served on commissions related to the broadcasting industry appointed by presidents Clinton and Bush; independent commissions focused on journalism and new media; and numerous newspaper industry boards. He has been recognized for his work on First Amendment and Freedom of Information initiatives, and is currently a member of Harvard University's Center for Ethics and the Board of Visitors of the Columbia University Graduate School of Journalism.

Dobbs, Lou—PAGE 143: Louis Dobbs was born on September 24, 1945, and is a CNN anchor and the managing editor for *Lou Dobbs Tonight*. He is an editorial columnist and syndicated radio show host and author of several books. Dobbs has won numerous major awards for his television journalism, most notably a Lifetime Achievement Emmy Award and a Cable Ace Award. He received the George Foster Peabody Award for his coverage of the 1987 stock market crash. He also received the Luminary Award of the Business Journalism Review in 1990, the Horatio Alger Association Award for Distinguished Americans in 1999, and the National Space Club Media Award in 2000. In 2004, Dobbs was awarded the Eugene Katz Award For Excellence in the Coverage of Immigration by the Center for Immigration Studies and in 2005 he received the Alexis de Tocqueville Institution's Statesmanship Award.

Dorsett, Tony—PAGE 132: Anthony "Tony" Drew Dorsett was born on April 7, 1954, in Rochester, Pennsylvania, and is a former running back in the National Football League for the Dallas Cowboys and the Denver Broncos. Tony was a running back from the University of Pittsburgh, and joined the Dallas Cowboys as their first-round draft pick in 1977. A four-time All-America at Pittsburgh, Dorsett also won the 1976 Heisman Trophy. He was a veteran of four Pro Bowls, and played in five NFC championship games and Super Bowls XII and XIII. In 1982 during a Monday night game against the Minnesota Vikings, Dorsett set a record that will never be broken—a ninety-nine-yard touchdown run. OUTTAKE **9** Tony Dorsett with his family, Jazmyn, 17, Madison, 10, and Mia, 5.

Eubank, Mary Grace—PAGE 188: Mary Grace Eubank is an illustrator's illustrator. She started her career illustrating greeting cards for such companies as Hallmark. Her work has appeared in *Sesame Street Magazine*. She supplied artwork for character profiles included in every volume of *Sesame Street Treasury* and also illustrated dozens of children's books including *Barney's Favorite Mother Goose Rhymes*. Mary Grace along with her husband, Ted, raise award-winning Cavalier King Charles Spaniels at their home in Copper Canyon, Texas. In February 2008, Mary Grace and Ted took the gold in best breed at the Westminster Dog Show in New York with their dog Rocky.

Fearing, Dean—PAGE 83: Dean Fearing is known as the "Father of Southwestern Cuisine." He is a graduate of the Culinary Institute of America. Dean is the creator and chef/partner of Fearing's Restaurant in Dallas, Texas, named Restaurant of the Year and Table of the Year by *Esquire Magazine* in 2007 and No. 1 in Hotel Dining in the U.S. by Zagat in 2009. Chef Fearing was presented with the April 2009 Silver Spoon Award for sterling performance by Food Arts, and he has also received a James Beard Foundation nomination for Best New Restaurant and was winner of the James Beard Foundation Restaurant Award for Best Chef in the Southwest.

Ferrare, Cristina—PAGE 64: Cristina Ferrare is a former fashion model, actress, author, and television talk-show host. She started a career in modeling at the age of sixteen with the Ford modeling agency in New York. Her career as a super model spanned over twenty-five years. Ferrare was the spokesperson for Max Factor between the ages of sixteen and twenty-six and a presenter on various television programs during the 1980s including *AM Los Angeles* and *Men Are From Mars, Women Are From Venus*. She has also written a number of books including *Cristina Ferrare's Family Entertaining, Okay, So I Don't Have a Headache*, and *Realistically Ever After*. In 2006, she started her own line of home accessories through her own company, Ferrare With Company. Cristina will start her own cooking show on Oprah Winfrey's network *OWN* in January 2010.

Fisher, Vernon—PAGE 187: Born in Texas in 1943, Vernon Fisher began making art on a professional basis in the 1970s. Influenced by Los Angeles artists Ed Ruscha, John Baldessari, and William Wegman, his attraction to mixed-media installations that combine written text, photography, and found objects links him to conceptual art. Fisher continues to live in Fort Worth with four cats and his wife, Julie Bozzi, who he suspects may also be a cat. OUTTAKE **10**

Force, Ashley—PAGE 36: Ashley Force Hood was born on November 29, 1982, and is a Funny Car drag racer. She is the daughter of fourteen-time NHRA Funny Car national champion John Force and his wife Laurie Force. She is married to Daniel Hood, who works for John Force Racing. Force was also selected as the NHRA POWERade Drag Racing Series' Rookie of the Year (Funny Car division) in November 2007. On April 27, 2008, Force earned her first ever NHRA professional win, defeating her father in the final round, and becoming the first woman to earn a win in the Funny Car class at the NHRA Summit Southern Nationals held at the Atlanta Dragway in Commerce, Georgia.

Ford, Willa—PAGE 60: Amanda Lee Williford-Modano was born on January 22, 1981, and is known professionally as Willa Ford, a singer, songwriter, model, television personality, and film actress. She became known in 2001 as the self-proclaimed "Bad Girl of Pop," when she released her debut album, *Willa Was Here*. Aside from her music career, Ford has acted in movies, hosted several reality television shows, posed for *Playboy* and competed on ABC's top-rated television show, *Dancing with the Stars*.

Friedman, Kinky—PAGE 156: Richard S. "Kinky" Friedman was born in 1944 and is a singer, songwriter, author, politician, and former columnist for *Texas Monthly*. Kinky graduated from The University of Texas at Austin in 1966 with a Bachelor of Arts, majoring in psychology. He was one of two independent candidates in the 2006 election for the office of governor of Texas. Receiving 12.6 percent of the vote, Friedman placed fourth in the six-person race. He also founded Utopia Animal Rescue Ranch, the mission of which is to care for stray, abused and aging animals. More than 1,000 dogs have been saved from animal euthanasia through the efforts of the ranch. OUTTAKE **11**

Gault, Sharon—PAGE 184: Sharon Gault, known as "Mama Makeup" from the nickname she earned while touring with Madonna for the *Blond Ambition* tour, is internationally known for her groundbreaking work with makeup. Sharon has created iconic looks for some of the biggest names in show business and fashion, and in the process, defined emerging trends for two decades in modern pop culture. Sharon's work has be featured in a variety of publications such as *Italian Vogue, British Vogue, Interview, The Face, Arena, Vanity Fair, ID, In-Style, Glamour, Allure, Marie Claire, GQ, Elle, W, Harper's & Queen*, and *Rolling Stone*.

Gilman, Dr. Alfred—PAGE 99: Alfred Goodman Gilman was born on July 1, 1941, and is a pharmacologist and biochemist. He shared the 1994 Nobel Prize in Physiology or Medicine with Martin Rodbell for their discoveries regarding G-proteins. Gilman graduated from Yale with his B.S. in 1962. He graduated Case Western Reserve University School of Medicine in Cleveland, Ohio, in 1969 with MD and PhD distinctions. Then did his post-doctoral studies at the National Institutes of Health with Nobel laureate Marshall Nirenberg from 1969 until 1971. In addition to winning the Nobel Prize, he won the Albert Lasker Award for Basic Medical Research as well as the Louisa Gross Horwitz Prize from Columbia University in 1989 together with Edwin Krebs, winner of Nobel Prize in medicine in 1992.

Graham, Jack—PAGE 107: Dr. Jack Graham was born on June 30, 1950, and is the pastor of Prestonwood Baptist Church. Jack earned a Bachelor of Science degree with honors from Hardin-Simmons University in Abilene, Texas. In 1976, he completed work for a Master of Divinity degree with honors from Southwestern Baptist Theological Seminary and in 1980, he received a Doctor of Ministry degree in "Church and Proclamation." In addition to being the pastor of Prestonwood Baptist, Jack is the voice of PowerPoint Ministries, the broadcast ministry of Prestonwood. Prestonwood is one of the largest congregations in the United States, with a membership exceeding 26,000.

 Green, Pat—PAGE 43: Patrick Craven (Pat) Green was born on April 5, 1972, in San Antonio, Texas, and is a country music artist. Active since 1995, he has recorded a total of ten studio albums, including several independent works—three for Republic Records and one for BNA. Fifteen of his singles have charted on the Billboard Hot Country Songs charts, of which the highest-peaking is the No. 3 *Wave on Wave* from his gold-certified album of the same name. OUTTAKE **12 13**

 Hartnett, Steve—PAGE 175: Steve Hartnett began his professional career with the opening of a pub in Lubbock, Texas, at the age of twenty-three. Since that time he has owned more than 250 restaurants—Fox and Hound, Cool River, III Forks, Bob's Steak and Chophouse, and Flips Patio Grill to name a few. While owning restaurants, he operates a highly successful money management firm that has been profitable for twenty-five of the last twenty-seven years. In fact if you had invested $1,000 in 1982 and not taken any distributions, it would be worth an astounding $14,567,422 in 2009. Numbers that make Warren Buffett envious. Hartnett and his wife, Sandy, have two children, Dionne and Taylor.

 Hickman, Sara—PAGE 103: Sara Hickman was born on March 1, 1963, and is a rock/folk/pop/children's music singer, songwriter, and artist. Hickman has released more than fifteen albums, including a half dozen on major record labels, and a few independent albums. She has been a guest performer on at least twenty-five albums by other musicians. She had a No. 3 adult contemporary hit *I Couldn't Help Myself,* has twice been a guest of NBC's *Tonight Show,* hosted her own VH-1 special, produced an independent video, *Joy,* that won first place in the USA Film Festival, and co-produced a PBS documentary titled *Take It Like A Man.* OUTTAKE **14**

 Hicks, Tom—PAGE 152: Thomas O. Hicks Sr. was born in Dallas, Texas, in 1946 and is a Dallas businessman with a bachelor's degree in finance from The University of Texas in 1968, and an MBA from the University of Southern California in 1970. Hicks is chairman of Hicks Holdings LLC, which owns and operates Hicks Sports Group, the company that owns the Texas Rangers, the Dallas Stars, and Mesquite Championship Rodeo. According to *Forbes Magazine* in 2009, Tom Hicks has an estimated wealth of one billion dollars.

 Horchow, Roger—PAGE 168 Samuel Roger Horchow was born on July 3, 1928, in Cincinnati, Ohio, and is a catalog entrepreneur and Broadway producer. In 1971, Horchow started the *Horchow Collection,* the first luxury mail-order catalog that was not preceded by a brick-and-mortar presence. He sold the *Horchow Collection* to Neiman Marcus in 1988. Horchow is a member of The Hill School Class of 1945. In 2002 he received the school's highest alumni honor, The Sixth Form Leadership Award. Horchow was awarded an honorary doctorate by his alma mater, Yale University, in 1999, and is a subject of *The Tipping Point* (Little, Brown, 2000) 2002 edition ISBN 0-316-34662-4, an influential book by *New Yorker* writer Malcolm Gladwell.

 Huddy, Juliet—PAGE 91: Juliet Ann Marie Huddy was born on September 27, 1969, and is a television news reporter, currently co-hosting the morning talk show *The Morning Show with Mike and Juliet.* Huddy currently works at the New York Fox News Studios, and resides in Hoboken, New Jersey, with her husband, Doug Barrett, her Chihuahua, Gomez, and her Bulldog, Lewis. OUTTAKE **15**

 Hughes, Karen—PAGE 124: Karen Parfitt Hughes was born on December 27, 1956, and is a Republican political adviser from the state of Texas. She served as the under secretary of state for public diplomacy and public affairs in the U.S. Department of State with the rank of ambassador. Hughes received her bachelor's degree from Southern Methodist University in 1977 where she was a member of Alpha Delta Pi sorority. She worked as a television news reporter from 1977 to 1984. In 1984, she went to work as the Texas press coordinator for the Reagan-Bush campaign in the 1984 election. She later became executive director of the Republican Party of Texas. She has been decorated by ABC News as Bush's "most essential advisor."

 Hunt, W. Herbert—PAGE 140: William Herbert Hunt, born March 6, 1929, grew up in the oil and gas industry. He received a degree in geology from Washington and Lee University in 1951 and was fortunate to work with numerous Hunt Family companies. Hunt was involved in the discovery and development of numerous giant oil fields, both domestically and internationally. He served the energy industry as past head of American Association of Drilling Contractors and National Ocean Industries Association and is presently on the board of the American Petroleum Institute and corporate advisory board of American Association of Petroleum Geologist. He was chosen as a member of All American Wildcat Committee and received Distinguished Service Award of Texas Mid-Continent Oil & Gas Association. Hunt and his wife, Nancy, their five children, sixteen grandchildren, and two great-grandchildren with more to come, are all involved in the family investments. When the clan gathers at Game Creek Ranch it includes sixteen dogs with Labs in preponderance. OUTTAKE **16** Herbert and Nancy Hunt with three of their dogs.

 Johnson, Jimmy—PAGE 67: James William Johnson was born on July 16, 1943, and is a former football coach who currently appears on *Fox NFL Sunday,* the FOX network's NFL pregame show. He attended college at the University of Arkansas and was an all-SWC defensive lineman on the 1964 National Championship football team. Johnson is one of only two head coaches to win both a college football national championship and a Super Bowl. Johnson coached the Dallas Cowboys to win two consecutive Super Bowls, Super Bowl XXVII in 1992 and Super Bowl XXVIII in 1993.

 Jones, Shirley—PAGE 44: Shirley Mae Jones was born on March 31, 1934, and is a singer and character actress of stage, film, and television. She starred as wholesome characters in a number of well-known musical films, such as *Oklahoma!, Carousel,* and *The Music Man.* She won the Academy Award for Best Supporting Actress for playing a prostitute in *Elmer Gantry.* She is probably best known as Shirley Partridge, the widowed mother of five children in the sitcom/television series *The Partridge Family,* co-starring her real-life stepson David Cassidy, son of Jack Cassidy. OUTTAKE **17**

Kelleher, Herb—PAGE 104 Herbert D. Kelleher is the founder and chairman emeritus of Dallas-based Southwest Airlines. Under his leadership, Southwest grew from a tiny intra-Texas carrier to one of America's best business success stories. He was born on March 12, 1931, in Haddon Heights, New Jersey, as the youngest of four children. He received his bachelor's degree from Wesleyan University and a law degree from New York University. Among his many achievements in business and aviation, Herb was inducted into the National Aviation Hall of Fame in 2008; received the Wright Brothers Memorial Trophy in 2000; was named one of history's top three CEOs by Chief Executive Magazine in 2005; and received the Steve Fossett Innovation Award in 2009.

 Lieberman, Nancy—PAGE 147: Nancy Ilizabeth Lieberman was born on July 1, 1958, in Brooklyn, New York. Nickname "Lady Magic," she is a Basketball Hall of Famer, two-time Olympian, three-time All-American, WNBA player for the Phoenix Mercury, former coach/GM for the Detroit Shock, acclaimed broadcaster for ESPN/ABC, motivational speaker, and esteemed writer and author. Lieberman is regarded as one of the greatest figures in women's basketball. In 1996 she was inducted into the Naismith Basketball Hall of Fame. Lieberman is a member of the Women's Basketball Hall of Fame, Virginia Sports Hall of Fame, Nassau County Hall of Fame, NYC Basketball Hall of Fame, and Hampton Roads Hall of Fame. On July 24, 2008, she made history again by playing in the WNBA, for the Detroit Shock at the age of fifty. www.nancylieberman.com, twitter.com/nancylieberman

 Loeb, Lisa—PAGE 52: Lisa Anne Loeb was born March 11, 1968, and is a singer, songwriter, and actress. She launched her career in 1994 with the Grammy-nominated, platinum-selling No. 1 hit song, *Stay (I Missed You)*. To this day, she is still the only artist to have a number one single while not signed to a recording contract. Her five acclaimed studio CDs include her major label debut, the gold-selling *Tails*, and its follow-up, the Grammy-nominated, gold-selling *Firecracker*. Lisa launched her own nonprofit, The Camp Lisa Foundation, designed to help underprivileged kids attend summer camp through its partnership with Summer Camp Opportunities Provide an Edge, Inc. (S.C.O.P.E.). Special thanks to Michelle Bankson for hair and makeup.

 Mack, Big Al—PAGE 180: Big Al Mack lives in Dallas, Texas, and is a radio personality and member of the *Kidd Kraddick in the Morning* radio show. The show is broadcast from 6 to 10 a.m. CST on weekday mornings and is nationally syndicated in sixty-two markets. Big Al was voted "Best Radio Show Sidekick" in the *Dallas Observer* reader's poll.

 Mahan, Larry—PAGE 127: Larry Mahan was born on November 21, 1942, in Salem, Oregon, and is a former rodeo champion. He won the title of World All-Around Rodeo Champion for five consecutive years from 1966 to 1970, and a sixth time in 1973. Mahan was inducted into the Pro Rodeo Hall of Fame in 1979, the National Cowboy and Western Heritage Museum's Rodeo Hall of Fame in 1966, and the Oregon Sports Hall of Fame in 1985. He was also World Bull Riding Champion in 1965 and 1967. After he retired from rodeo, he established the Larry Mahan Collection, a line of western wear. OUTTAKE**18** Larry Mahan poses with photographers Richard Michael Pruitt and David Woo.

 Marion, Anne Windfohr—PAGE 76: Anne Windfohr Marion was born on November 10, 1938, and is the chairman of Burnett Oil Co., Inc, the president of Burnett Ranches, Ltd., and the president of the Burnett Foundation. She attended Miss Porters School in Farmington, Connecticut, and Briarcliff Junior College, Briarcliff, New York. Her great grandfather, Samuel Burk Burnett, established the 6666 Ranch in Texas. She is an emeritus trustee of Texas Christian University, trustee of The Kimbell Art Foundation, trustee of Modern Art Museum of Fort Worth, and an honorary vice president of both The American Quarter Horse Association and the Fort Worth Stock Show. She is the director of Texas and Southwestern Cattle Raisers Association, director emeritus of the National Cowboy Hall of Fame, and chairman of the board of directors of The Georgia O'Keeffe Museum. Her honors are many, including being inducted into the National Cowgirl Hall of Fame in 2005 and the American Quarter Horse Associate Hall of Fame in March 2007. She received the Museum of New Mexico Foundation Award for Outstanding Philanthropy in May 2007, and was inducted into The Great Hall of Westerners National Cowboy and Western Heritage Museum April 2009.

 Marven, Nigel—PAGE 39: Nigel Marven, born November 27, 1960, is a British wildlife presenter, television producer, author, and ornithologist. Known for his unorthodox, spontaneous, and daring style of presenting wildlife documentaries, in his first television series for ITV, *Giants*, he swam with a great white shark without the protection of a cage. OUTTAKE**19**

 McGraw, Jay—PAGE 55: Jay Phillip McGraw was born on September 12, 1979, and is the son of Phil McGraw (also known as Dr. Phil) and Robin McGraw. Jay earned his law degree from Southern Methodist University, and is a graduate of The University of Texas, where he received a B.S. in psychology. He has written several books aimed at young people, which are based on his famous father's books. Jay has also appeared on Dr. Phil's TV show. He is president and CEO of Stage 29 Productions in Los Angeles and is executive producer of the TV series *The Doctors*, which is an advice show in which four doctors discuss various medical topics. OUTTAKE**20** Jay and his wife Erica with their cat Bizant.

 Millan, Cesar—PAGE 24: Cesar Millan was born on August 27, 1969, and is a professional dog trainer. In his words, he "rehabilitates dogs, trains people." He is best known for his television series *Dog Whisperer*, which is currently in its fifth season and airs on the *National Geographic Channel* in the U.S., *BIO* in Australia, and on *Sky 3* in the UK. He is also the co-author of the best selling books *Cesar's Way, Be the Pack Leader* and *A Member of the Family*. The International Association of Canine Professionals awarded Cesar and his wife, Ilusion, with honorary membership in March 2006.

 Miller, Jan—PAGE 15: Jan Miller has been called "a supernova in a galaxy of literary agents." As founder and CEO one of the top literary agencies in the country, Dupree/Miller & Associates, she has used her unwavering instincts to yield thousands of international best-sellers across all genres. Her success has made Dupree/Miller a driving force in the publishing industry—an agency that represents blockbuster authors, innovators, and brands across all genres.

 Miller, Steve—PAGE 27: Steve Miller was born on October 5, 1943, in Milwaukee, Wisconsin, where he was given his first lessons in guitar by Les Paul at age five and was raised in Texas where T-Bone Walker taught him to play lead guitar at the age of nine. Steve is a guitarist and singer/songwriter and leader of the Steve Miller Band. Beginning his career in blues and rock in San Francisco, Miller created an original Texas flavored music which earned him multi-platinum success with a series of successful singles and albums from the mid-1970s to today, including *Gangster of Love, Space Cowboy, Fly Like An Eagle, Rock'n Me, Take the Money and Run, Jet Airliner, Jungle Love,* and *Abracadabra*. Miller's greatest hits album was recently certified at eighteen million copies, placing him in the top echelon of all recording artists. OUTTAKE**21 22**

 Minick, Pam—PAGE 171: Pam has been a champion calf roper, actress, movie stuntperson, businesswoman and sports commentator. She served as vice president of the WPRA helping to bring about significant advances for women's rodeo. She was also a popular national rodeo spokeswoman helping increase the popularity of her sport. Pam is a Former Miss Rodeo America, a World Champion Breakaway Roper, a Lane Frost Award Winner, and a Tad Lucas Award Winner. OUTTAKE**23 24**

Mizrahi, Isaac—PAGE 40: Born in Brooklyn, New York, Isaac Mizrahi's passion for design and performance began at an early age. Isaac studied acting at the High School of Performing Arts and Fashion Design at Parsons. As creative director for the Liz Claiborne brand, Isaac oversees design and marketing for the women's apparel and accessories line. Mizrahi has been awarded four CFDA awards. Available domestically and internationally, Isaac's women's collection can be seen in fashion magazines around the globe. Currently, Isaac is the host of the Bravo television series *The Fashion Show.* Isaac shoots a web series on www.watchisaac.com and wrote his first book *How to Have Style,* released October 2008. OUTTAKE 25 26

 Modano, Mike—PAGE 47: Michael Thomas Modano, Jr. was born on June 7, 1970, in Livonia, Michigan, and is a professional ice hockey player and alternate captain for the Dallas Stars of the National Hockey League (NHL). He is the all-time goal-scoring and points leader among American-born players in the NHL. Modano won the Stanley Cup in 1999 with the Stars. He is the founder and current vice president of the Mike Modano Foundation, Inc., which raises awareness and funding for organizations offering education and assistance to children and families affected by child abuse

 Murray, Ty—PAGE 31: Ty Monroe Murray was born on October 1, 1969, and is a nine-time World Champion rodeo cowboy and co-founder and board adviser of the Professional Bull Riders. At 20 he became the youngest rider ever to win the PRCA All-Around World Championship, also the first to win both the PRCA All-Around and NIRA Men's titles the same year. Murray won the PRCA World Bull Riding Championship title in 1993 and 1998. Murray retired from rodeo in 2002 and is currently the president of the PBR. He was also a contestant on the eighth season of *Dancing with the Stars.* OUTTAKE 27 28 29

 Neary, Lynn—PAGE 155: Lynn Neary is a radio journalist. She is a correspondent on National Public Radio and on National Desk's Arts and Information Unit, covering books and publishing. She earned a B.A. in english from Fordham University in New York. She won the Robert F. Kennedy Journalism Award in 1988 for *635 K Street.* In 1992 she won the Corporation for Public Broadcasting Gold Award, an Ohio State Award, and an Association for Women Radio and Television Award for her reporting on *A Primer on Breast Cancer.* Neary also received the 1994–95 Alfred I. duPont-Columbia University Silver Baton Award for her reporting on welfare reform. She also won a 1999 Gabriel Award for her report on a program for prisoners in New York's Sing Sing prison.

 Nelson, Byron—PAGE 135: John Byron Nelson, Jr. was born on February 4, 1912, and died on September 26, 2006. Nelson was a PGA Tour golfer between 1935 and 1946, retiring at age 34. Nelson lended his name to the HP Byron Nelson Championship, the first PGA Tour event to be named for a professional golfer. In 1974, Byron received the Bob Jones Award, the highest honor given by the United States Golf Association in recognition of distinguished sportsmanship in golf. He became the second recipient of the PGA Tour Lifetime Achievement Award in 1997, and was inducted into the World Golf Hall of Fame in 1974. He received the 1994 Old Tom Morris Award from the Golf Course Superintendents Association of America, GCSAA's highest honor. Nelson received the Congressional Gold Medal shortly after his death in 2006. OUTTAKE 30 Byron Nelson's wife Peggy helps position Peppy.

 Nelson, Don—PAGE 160: Donald Arvid Nelson was born on May 15, 1940, in Muskegon, Michigan, and is a former National Basketball Association player and currently is the head coach of the Golden State Warriors. He has also coached the Milwaukee Bucks, the New York Knicks, and the Dallas Mavericks. An innovator, Nelson is credited with inventing the concept of the point forward, a tactic which is frequently employed by teams at every level today. His unique brand of basketball is often referred to as "Nellie Ball." He is considered one of the Top ten coaches in NBA history. OUTTAKE 31

 Ordon, Dr. Andrew—PAGE 136: Andrew Ordon is a plastic and reconstructive surgeon with private practices in California, as well as the Assistant Clinical Professor of Plastic Surgery at Dartmouth Medical College and UCLA School of Medicine. He graduated from USC School of Medicine, UCLA, and Loma Linda University School of Medicine. He went on to complete his training in plastic and reconstructive surgery at the Lenox Hill Hospital and the Manhattan Eye and Ear Infirmary Program in New York City. Dr. Ordon is on *The Doctors,* which is executive produced by Jay McGraw. He is the author of *Revealing the New You: A Guide to Plastic Surgery* and *Everything You Always Wanted to Know About Plastic Surgery* and has been featured on the following TV shows: *Plastic Surgery Today, Dr. Phil, Entertainment Tonight, 20/20, NBC Nightly News,* and *ABC World News.* OUTTAKE 32

 Paige, Ashley—PAGE 139: Ashley Paige is a swimwear designer and businesswoman. Her styles have graced the pages of numerous magazines as well as countless television appearances including *Extra, ET, The Style Network, MTV, VH1,* and Bravo. Ashley uses the spotlight to promote animal rescue and is know to bring homeless dogs down the runway and wears t-shirts reading "Save a stray." Ashley also hosts weekly pet adoptions at her boutique-studio in Hollywood. Special thanks to celebrity makeup artist Sharon Gault and her stylist Harry McDaniel. OUTTAKE 33 34

 Parker, Fess—PAGE 128: Fess Elisha Parker, Jr. was born on August 16, 1924, and is a film and television actor best known for his 1950s portrayals of Davy Crockett for Walt Disney and of Daniel Boone in the late 1960s. He graduated from the University of Texas in 1950 with a history degree and went on to study drama at the University of Southern California. Currently, Fess is a winemaker and resort owner-operator.

 Patterson, Carly—PAGE 71: Carly Rae Patterson was born on February 4, 1988, in Baton Rouge, Louisiana, and is a former gymnast. She is the 2004 Olympic All-Around Gymnastics Champion and a member of the USA Gymnastics Hall of Fame. She currently lives in Allen, Texas. On February 4, 2008, Carly signed a recording contract with Music Mind Records, a Chicago based Indie label. Her first single *Temporary Life (Ordinary Girl)* was released on March 25, 2008.

 Phil, Dr.—PAGE 20: Phillip Calvin McGraw was born on September 1, 1950, and graduated in 1975 from Midwestern State University with a Bachelor of Arts degree in psychology and later earned a master's degree in experimental psychology in 1976, and a PhD in clinical psychology in 1979 at the University of North Texas. McGraw is best known as Dr. Phil, an American television personality, author, and former psychologist, currently the host of his own television show, *Dr. Phil.* OUTTAKE 35

 Pickens, T. Boone—PAGE 123 Thomas Boone Pickens, Jr. was born on May 22, 1928, in Holdenville, Oklahoma, and chairs the hedge fund BP Capital Management. He was a well-known takeover operator during the 1980s. Pickens received the 2009 Bower Award for Business Leadership for fifty years of visionary leadership in oil and other types of energy production, including domestic renewable energy, and for his philanthropic leadership contributing to education, medical research, and wildlife conservation. With an estimated current net worth of about three billion dollars, he is ranked by *Forbes* as the 117th-richest person in America and ranked 369th in the world. OUTTAKE 36

Pilgrim, Bo—PAGE 163: Lonnie "Bo" Pilgrim is the founder, chairman, and principal owner of Pilgrim's Pride, the largest chicken producer in the United States with the capacity to process more than nine billion pounds of poultry per year. Pilgrim founded Pilgrim's Pride when he opened a feed store in 1946 in Pittsburg, Texas, with his older brother, Aubrey. Today, Pilgrim's Pride is a Fortune 500 company with $8.5 billion in annual net sales and approximately 41,000 employees.

Rachofsky, Howard—PAGE 172: A successful money manager for more than thirty years (now retired), Howard Rachofsky is among the most recognized collectors of contemporary art. He is also one of Dallas' most involved and generous art patrons. Along with his wife, Cindy, he hosts *2x2 for Aids and Art* in their Richard Meier-designed home. Over the past decade this event has been among the most successful museum benefits in the U.S. For their efforts, Cindy and Howard received the Skowhegan Award presented for philanthropy in the arts. Howard was also honored in 2005 with the TACA Award, one of the most prestigious awards given to patrons of the visual and performing arts in Dallas. In addition to his patronage of the Dallas Museum of Art, Howard is a member of the board of DIA Art Foundation in New York. He also serves on the board of the Dallas Symphony Association and the Dallas Center for the Performing Arts, the Investment Committee of St. Phillip's School in Dallas and is a member of the board of directors of East Dallas Community School.

Rasberry, Kellie—PAGE 96: Angela Kellie Rasberry was born on April 13, 1967, and is a co-host of the radio talk show *Kidd Kraddick in the Morning* along with Kidd Kraddick, Big Al Mack, "Psycho" Shanon and J-Si. The show is broadcast from 6 to 10 a.m. CST on weekday mornings and is nationally syndicated in sixty-two markets. She graduated from Francis Marion University in 1993 with a Bachelors in Arts in the field of English.

Rehm, Diane—PAGE 28: Diane Rehm was born on September 21, 1936, in Washington, D.C., and is a public radio talk show host and published author. Her program, *The Diane Rehm Show,* is distributed nationally and internationally by National Public Radio. Read Diane's complete biography on page 207.

Richardson, Daryl—PAGE 95: As founder and director of The Dallas World Aquarium, Daryl Richardson sees it as his role to educate people about the importance of conservation for the earth's fragile ecosystems, such as coral reefs and rainforests. After graduating from the University of Texas with a major in marketing and advertising, he became a successful Dallas caterer, prior to his purchase of abandoned warehouses and a run-down parking lot in the downtown West End Historical District. These acquisitions were transformed into The Dallas World Aquarium (opened in 1992), the only for-profit, private zoo both accredited by the Association of Zoos and Aquariums (AZA) and the World Association of Zoos and Aquariums (WAZA). The DWA is now a leader in Central and South America Conservation efforts.

Romano, Phil—PAGE 148: Phillip J. Romano serves as co-chief executive officer of eatZi's Market & Bakery. He is an investor, entrepreneur, and nationally renowned restaurateur. He has been involved in the restaurant business for forty years and has created more than twenty different concepts including six national concept restaurants, more than anyone else in the industry. He and his family established a charitable foundation, The Food Foundation, which operates as Hunger Busters, and provides food to the hungry and has a mission of bringing a fresh meal with compassion to the hungry citizens of Dallas. OUTTAKE 37

Ryan, Nolan—PAGE 80: Lynn Nolan Ryan, Jr. was born on January 31, 1947, in Refugio, Texas, and is a retired Major League Baseball pitcher and current president of the Texas Rangers. Ryan played in a major-league-record twenty-seven seasons for the New York Mets, California Angels, Houston Astros, and Texas Rangers, from 1966 to 1993. Ryan is the all-time leader in no-hitters with seven, three more than any other pitcher. He is tied with Bob Feller for the most one-hitters, with twelve. Ryan also pitched eighteen two-hitters. Ryan was an eight-time MLB All-Star, and his 5,714 career strikeouts rank first in baseball history. He was inducted into the Baseball Hall of Fame in 1999.

Solomon, Andrew—PAGE 72: Andrew Solomon is the author of *The Irony Tower: Soviet Artists in a Time of Glasnost,* the novel *A Stone Boat,* and *The Noonday Demon: An Atlas of Depression,* which won the 2001 National Book Award, was a Pulitzer Prize finalist, and has now been published in twenty-four languages. He is a lecturer in psychiatry at Weill-Cornell Medical College, and a fellow of Berkeley College at Yale University. He writes regularly for *The New York Times, The New Yorker, Artforum,* and numerous other publications. His philanthropic interests include the arts, mental health, and gay civil rights. He lives in New York and London and is a dual national. OUTTAKE 38

Staubach, Roger—PAGE 59: Roger Thomas Staubach, also known as Roger the Dodger, Captain Comeback, and Captain America, was born on February 5, 1942, in Cincinnati, Ohio, and is a businessman, Heisman Trophy winner and legendary Hall of Fame quarterback for the Dallas Cowboys from 1969 until 1979. Staubach was key in developing the Cowboys to become America's Team and led the team to nine of the Cowboys record-setting twenty consecutive winning seasons. Staubach led the Cowboys to their first Super Bowl victory and as a result he was named MVP in Super Bowl VI. Staubach was described by legendary coach Tom Landry as "possibly the best combination of a passer, an athlete and a leader to ever play in the NFL."

Storm, Hannah—PAGE 164: Hannah Storm was born Hannah Storen on June 13, 1962, in Oak Park, Illinois, and is a journalist, author, television personality and the co-anchor of ESPN's *SportsCenter.* From 2002 until 2007, Storm was one of the hosts of CBS's *The Early Show.* She graduated from the University of Notre Dame in 1983, with degrees in political science and communications. Storm also created the Hannah Storm Foundation in 2008 to raise awareness and provide treatment for children suffering from debilitating and disfiguring vascular birthmarks.

Sullenberger, Chelsey "Sully"—PAGE 19: Chelsey Burnett "Sully" Sullenberger III was born on January 23, 1951, and is an airline transport pilot (ATP), safety expert, and accident investigator from Danville, California. Sullenberger successfully carried out the emergency ditching of US Airways Flight 1549 in the Hudson River, offshore from Manhattan, New York City, on January 15, 2009, thus saving the lives of the 155 people on the aircraft. He is an international speaker on airline safety and has helped develop new protocols for airline safety. Sullenberger graduated from the United States Air Force Academy and later earned a masters degree from Purdue University and has been awarded the Master's Medal from the Guild of Air Pilots and Air Navigators, the Key to the City from The City of New York, and the Jabara Award for Airmanship from the USAF Academy. OUTTAKE 39 Sully with his wife, Lorrie, and their dog, Twinkle.

Summerall, Pat—PAGE 100: George Allen "Pat" Summerall was born on May 10, 1930, in Lake City, Florida, and is a former professional football player and television sportscaster, having worked at CBS, FOX, and ESPN. Summerall is best known for his work with John Madden on CBS and FOX's NFL telecasts, and in 1999 he was inducted into the American Sportscasters Association Hall of Fame.

Thomas, B. J.—PAGE 63: Billy Joe Thomas was born August 7, 1942, in Hugo, Oklahoma, and is a popular singer known for his chart-topping hits in the 1960s and 1970s. Over the four decades B.J. Thomas has performed, he has sold more than seventy million records, earned two platinum records, has eleven gold records, won five Grammy Awards, two Dove Awards for Gospel recordings and fifteen Top 40 Pop/Rock Hits including: *Raindrops Keep Fallin' On My Head, Eyes Of A New York Woman, Hooked On A Feeling, Rock and Roll Lullaby,* and *I Just Can't Help Believing.*

Wade, Bob—PAGE 68: Bob "Daddy-O" Wade was born in Austin, Texas, the second cousin of Roy Rogers, growing up a hotel brat in places like Marfa and making hot rods in places like El Paso. The "artiste of Tex-Mex" snagged beers, fun, and art degrees from University of Texas Austin and The University of California, Berkeley. Bob was awarded three NEA Grants and was in Biennials in New Orleans, Paris, and the Whitney Museum in New York. He is in numerous museum, corporate, and private collections throughout the US and Europe. It is his large scale public sculptures such as the forty-foot Cowboy Boots in San Antonio, the seveny-foot Saxophone in Houston, the twelve-foot Dancing Frogs south of Dallas, and the twenty-five-foot Sombrero Man in Malibu that have put Bob on the pop culture map. Only an artist who put the forty-foot Iguana on the roof of New York's Lone Star Café would put a lizard on his head for this book.

Robert Wagner—PAGE 48: One of the most popular and successful stars in the entertainment industry, Robert Wagner has had a career highlighted by three hit television series and an impressive portfolio of movies for film and television as well as becoming a best-selling author. While Wagner was still a young man under contract to Twentieth Century Fox, Darryl F. Zanuck cast him in *With a Song in My Heart.* The part was perhaps a minute's duration, but in that minute, the tears pouring from Wagner's eyes as he played the role of a crippled soldier responding to the singing of Miss Hayward's Jane Froman, brought immediate reaction pouring into the studio from the public. That one-minute part established Wagner as a major star, and he has been working ever since. In the fall of 2008, Wagner wrote his memoir, *Pieces of My Heart* for Harper Collins, debuting at No. 3 on the *New York Times* best-seller list . The book provides an inside look at his life and career, from his days as a teen caddying for Clark Gable, to his friendships with some of the biggest Hollywood names of our time. "Special thanks to Susan Flynn, my professional dog trainer, owner of, Aspen Dog Training in Aspen, Colorado," said Wagner. "She was there on our photo shoot helping me with Max."

Walker, Jerry Jeff—PAGE 35: Jerry Jeff Walker was born on March 16, 1942, and is a country music singer. Born Ronald Clyde Crosby in Oneonta, New York, he moved to Austin, Texas, in the 1970s, associating mainly with the country-rock outlaw scene. With thirty albums, Jerry Jeff Walker is a talented musician and may be most well known for his song *Mr. Bojangles.* In 1999 he published an autobiography, *Gypsy Songman,* accompanied by an LP of the same name

Wardy, Amen—PAGE 116: Having made his mark on the world of exclusive women's couture with glittering boutiques in Texas, Beverly Hills and Newport Beach, California, in the mid-90s, Amen Wardy, the renowned specialty retailer, expanded his affinity for luxury retailing into a home furnishing, gourmet and gift boutique. Amen Wardy, the creative genius behind Amen Wardy Home has been instrumental in creating an entirely new perspective in home design and entertaining since 1954. The Amen Wardy Home collection captures the essence of modern inspired living with uniqueness of design, creative entertaining, versatility, and above all, luxury. OUTTAKES **40 41**

Waters, Charlie—PAGE 112: Charlie Tutan Waters was born on September 10, 1948, in Miami, Florida, and is a former football safety for the Dallas Cowboys from 1970–81 in the National Football League. He spent one season (2006) as a radio broadcaster for the Dallas Cowboys radio network. He was selected All-Pro twice (1977 and 1978) and to the Pro Bowl three consecutive seasons (1976–78). Waters played in five Super Bowls: V, VI, X, XII, and XIII, with victories in VI and XII.

White, Ron—PAGE 56: Ron White was born on December 18, 1956, and is a Grammy Award-nominated stand-up comedian from Fritch, Texas. He was a member of the *Blue Collar Comedy Tour* along with Jeff Foxworthy, Bill Engvall, and Larry the Cable Guy. Other than the *Blue Collar Comedy Tour* CDs and movies, White has released five solo projects of his own as well as writing a book titled *I Had the Right to Remain Silent ... But I Didn't Have the Ability* which mixes material from his stand-up act with stories from his youth. OUTTAKE **42** Ron White with his wife, Margo Reymundo.

Whitworth, Kathy—PAGE 179: Kathy Whitworth was born on September 27, 1939, in Monahans, Texas, and is a professional golfer. Throughout her playing career she won eighty-eight LPGA Tour tournaments, more than anyone else has won on either the LPGA Tour or the PGA Tour. In 1981 she became the first woman to reach career earnings of one million dollars on the LPGA Tour. Kathy is a Member of the Women's Sports Foundation Hall of Fame and the World Golf Hall of Fame. Special thanks to Marisha Teagardin of Advanced K9 Concepts and Jenifer Batchelder of Dallas/Fort Worth Labrador Retriever Rescue Club, Inc. OUTTAKE **43**

Wilson, Owen—PAGE 12: Owen Cunningham Wilson was born November 18, 1968, in Dallas, Texas, and is a successful actor, comedian and writer. Wilson's parents are photographer Laura Cunningham Wilson and Robert Andrew Wilson, an advertising executive and operator of a public television station. He has an older brother, Andrew and a younger brother, Luke, both also involved in filmmaking. Wilson got his big break with the 2000 comedy action hit *Shanghai Noon,* starring opposite Hong Kong action star Jackie Chan. The film grossed nearly one hundred million dollars worldwide. He has gone on to appear or star in more than thirty films including *Behind Enemy Lines, The Royal Tenenbaums, Zoolander, Starsky and Hutch, Wedding Crashers, Night at the Museum,* and *Marlee and Me* to name a few. OUTTAKE **44 45** Owen Wilson and Suzi Woo.

Wilson, Trisha—PAGE 16: Trisha Wilson is the founder and chief executive officer of Wilson Associates, an interior architectural design firm based in Dallas, Texas, with six other offices spanning the globe. The firm was founded in 1971 and employs a staff of over 350 professionals. Trisha Wilson is a dynamic businesswoman and an internationally acclaimed hotel designer who has built her global empire around the business of designing hotels, restaurants, clubs, casinos, and high-end residences. Wilson Associates is consistently ranked as one of the top firms in the hospitality design industry worldwide. Business associates describe Ms. Wilson as tireless, energetic, and enthusiastic. She is the chairman and founder of The Wilson Foundation, established to provide educational and health program support in South Africa.

Ziglar, Zig—PAGE 191: Hilary Hinton "Zig" Ziglar was born on November 6, 1926, and is an author, salesperson, and motivational speaker. He is an expert salesperson, best-selling author, and highly sought-after public speaker. Ziglar has a unique philosophy that stems from his own religious beliefs along with positive thinking. Selected published books by Zig Ziglar include *Better Than Good: Creating a Life You Can't Wait to Live, Confessions of a Grieving Christian, Zig Ziglar's Secrets of Closing the Sale, Success for Dummies, Over The Top,* and *See You at the Top,* to name a few.

Contributor Biographies

Diane Rehm began her radio career in 1973 as a volunteer producer for WAMU 88.5, the NPR member-station in Washington, D.C. She was hired and later became the host and producer of two health-oriented programs. In 1979, she began hosting WAMU's local morning talk show, *Kaleidoscope,* which was renamed *The Diane Rehm Show* in 1984.

Each week, more than 2.2 million listeners across the country tune in to *The Diane Rehm Show,* which has grown from a small local morning call-in show to one of public broadcasting's most popular programs, heard on more than 135 stations nationwide and distributed by National Public Radio, NPR Worldwide, and SIRIUS XM satellite radio. In 2008, *The Diane Rehm Show* was named to the list of the ten most powerful programs in public radio, based on its ability to draw listeners to public radio stations. The program was the only live call-in talk show in the list.

In 1998, Rehm's career nearly ended because of spasmodic dysphonia, a neurological voice disorder that causes strained, difficult speech. Rehm sought treatment, returned to the show, and called attention to the condition. The National Council on Communicative Disorders recognized her work with a Communication Award, and ABC's Nightline devoted an entire program to a conversation with Rehm about her disorder.

Rehm also is a successful author of two autobiographical books: *Finding My Voice* (Knopf, 1999), in which she describes her childhood, marriage, career, and voice disorder; and *Toward Commitment: A Dialogue about Marriage* (Knopf, 2002), a deeply personal book co-written with her husband, John.

Many of the nation's prominent newsmakers, journalists, and authors have appeared on her show, including then-Sen. Barack Obama, former presidents Bill Clinton and Jimmy Carter, former Vice President Dick Cheney, former Secretary of State Colin Powell, retired Supreme Court Justice Sandra Day O'Connor, Sen. John McCain (R-Az.), Nobel Laureate and Pulitzer Prize-winning author Toni Morrison, and photographer Annie Leibovitz. National Journal calls Rehm "the class act of the talk radio world."

Rehm lives in Washington, D.C., with her husband, John, and their six-year-old long-haired Chihuahua, Maxie (short for Maximillian).

Maxie, who Diane calls the "king of the roost," has grown from a dog that would only play in his own garden and take walks in a stroller into one of the friendliest dogs in the neighborhood. He frequently accompanies Diane to work and guards her desk while she's on the air.

Richard Michael Pruitt recently completed forty years as a photographer for *The Dallas Morning News* where he had several positions including *Sunday Magazine* photographer, director of photography and senior staff photographer. Pruitt has received awards from numerous organizations for his photography and was on the staff that won the 2006 Pulitzer for their coverage of Hurricane Katrina. His work has been published in *Time, Newsweek, People,* and the former *Life Magazine.* In recent years, Pruitt has been video storytelling for various companies and organizations. Richard is currently working on an untitled nature documentary in East Texas.

Pruitt lives in Dallas with his wife, Sandra, of forty-five years. They have two grown children, Michelle Pruitt Taylor and Brian Pruitt, and four grandchildren, Zachery, Nicholas, Peyton, and Gavin.

PHOTO BY STEVE MILLER

David Woo is a two-time Pulitzer Prize finalist who studied at the University of Texas at Austin and received a Bachelor of Journalism degree in photojournalism in 1976. In 2006, with the photography staff of *The Dallas Morning News,* he won the Pulitzer Prize for Breaking News Photography. He helped produce *The Eyes of the Storm, Hurricanes Katrina and Rita: The Photographic Story.* He is the winner of eleven Texas Katie Awards from the Press Club of Dallas for his photography. In 1988, he was a finalist for Photographer of the Year, sponsored by the National Press Photographers Association. He has been employed with *The Dallas Morning News* for over thirty-three years. In addition to his newspaper work, David is a published photographer in a wide range of national and international magazines including *Life, Time, Newsweek, Parade Magazine, People, Sports Illustrated, GQ, Vanity Fair, Esquire,* and *Texas Monthly,* to name a few. His popular coffee table portrait book, *Texas Women,* published in 1984 with fellow *The Dallas Morning News* photographer, Richard Pruitt, received national praise. The Corbis Photo Agency in New York City has represented him for the past thirty-three years. His work has been auctioned at the Modern Art Museum of Fort Worth and collected by many people who enjoy his artistic eye.

Woo lives in Arlington, Texas with his wife, Suzi. They have a blended family of five children, Zach, Jake, Carrie, Hilary and Shelby, two grandsons, Walker and Hughes, and one Bassett Hound—Chester.

Suzi Woo earned her Bachelor of Arts degree in art history from the University of California, Berkeley, and began her museum career at the Longview Museum and Art Center. Currently, Suzi is Director of Membership and Special Events at the Modern Art Museum of Fort Worth, a management position she has enjoyed for twenty-seven years. As a member of the Advisory Committee for Art Museum Membership Conference, she collaborates with other museum colleagues to create and facilitate the annual AMMC national conference, an organization she has been involved with throughout her career. During her free time Suzi writes travel features; travels with family, including her daughters Hilary Bowerman and Shelby Poole; and spends most cherished times with grandsons Walker and Hughes Bowerman.

Cesar and Ilusion Millan Foundation

Working directly with animal shelters and rescue organizations across the United States, the Cesar and Ilusion Millan Foundation supports the rescue, rehabilitation, and re-homing of abused and abandoned dogs. In addition to awarding grants to qualified organizations, the Foundation creates and delivers to children and communities humane education programs that nurture life-long healthy relationships between dogs and people.

Grant-Making Priorities:

The Cesar and Ilusion Millan Foundation provides financial support to assist non-profit animal shelters and organizations engaged in the rescuing, rehabilitation, and re-homing of abused and abandoned dogs. The Foundation prioritizes funding on spaying and neutering programs to help reduce or eliminate dog overpopulation.

Education Programs:

Shelter Stars, the Cesar and Ilusion Millan Foundation's animal shelter affiliation program, promotes positive, healthy relationships between families and the dogs they adopt from re-homing organizations across the country. Currently, *Shelter Stars* partners are distributing copies of "People Training for Dogs" (the most popular volume in Cesar Millan's "Mastering Leadership" DVD series) free of charge to families that adopt shelter dogs.

"Spay & Neuter is Nothing to Whisper About" is the Cesar and Ilusion Millan Foundation's public service campaign that includes television commercials, full color posters, and reproducible ads featuring messages from the "Dog Whisperer" himself to promote the importance of spaying and neutering dogs to curb overpopulation.

"The Foundation, which has long been a dream of ours, is intended to benefit needy shelters and rescue organizations throughout the United States. Our many years of experience in the rehabilitation of dogs of every breed and background has taught us that most animals can make excellent companions, and all that many of them need is the proper care and a second chance."

- Cesar and Ilusion Millan

MillanFoundation.org

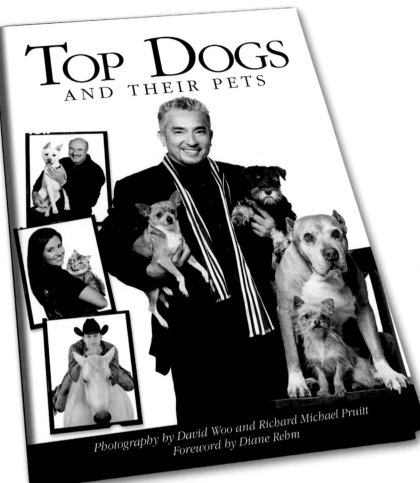

More About Top Dogs And Their Pets

For special offers and to order additional copies of *Top Dogs and Their Pets*
visit the official website **www.TopDogsPets.com**

To learn more about the book, the authors, and to see exclusive videos of the "Top Dogs"
featured in the book visit **www.TopDogsPets.com** today.

To inquire about this book, order bulk quantities of the book, or request more information
please contact Pediment Publishing at 360-687-6731 extension 109.

Portions of the proceeds from *Top Dogs and Their Pets* will go directly to the
Cesar & Ilusion Millan Foundation, which offers financial support and rehabilitation
expertise to pet shelters and rescue organizations throughout the United States.